Contents

Preface

The idea for this book was developed by the 1990 Association for Library Service to Children (ALSC) Publications Committee, chaired by Sue McCleaf Nespeca and consisting of Kathleen Staerkel, Evelyn Walker, June Kahler, and Marilyn Hollingshead. Once the ALSC Board accepted the proposal, Sue and Kathy were asked to "line up" prospective authors to write the various chapters. We did this by contacting members of the ALSC Managing Children's Services Committee and the Managing Children's Services Discussion Group. Through the people involved in these two groups we began the process of networking through the ALSC organization to find people to write this book. One name led to another and eventually we had a list of people who enthusiastically supported the project and committed their talents and time to turn our idea into a reality.

As this work progressed, some of the topics and authors changed, yet the book remains fairly true to the original proposal. Our vision for this publication was a collection of essays written by persons who are knowledgeable about management issues through experience or education. As you read through each chapter you will find that this is so.

When the first drafts arrived for editing, Sue suggested that Mary Fellows be asked to assist us with the editing process because of her experience in both management and youth services. Luckily she agreed. Several phone calls later and a weekend in Ohio led to a division of manuscripts and the first revisions on the chapters.

Many thanks to the thirteen authors for contributing their expertise—Melody Lloyd Allen, Kathleen Deerr, Sherry Des Enfants, Floyd C. Dickman, Mary Fellows, Yvette Johnson, Marie C. Orlando, Maria B. Salvadore, Kathleen Staerkel, Kathy Toon, Mary M. Wagner, Virginia Walter, and Gretchen Wronka; to my co-editors—Sue McCleaf Nespeca and Mary Fellows; to Bonnie Smothers from ALA Editions; to Eileen Fitzsimons of ALA/ALSC; and to the ALSC members who led us to these experts in the field. Their commitment and hard work have led to a useful resource for youth services managers.

KATHLEEN STAERKEL

Introduction

In these days of rapidly evolving technology, of sweeping societal changes, and of ever-increasing government regulations, we are called on to be different professionals than we were even a few years ago. Gone are the days when the children's librarian concerned herself with selecting books, reading those books to children, and checking them out so that those tots or others could take them home. The children's librarian of today is likely to be called a youth services librarian, and is as apt to concern herself—or himself—with managing employees, administering a budget, developing policies, or writing grants as with reading stories to children, although that may still be a cherished part of each youth services librarian's week.

We are becoming this new breed of management-oriented professional because we must; because we understand that by not doing so we relinquish power to those who may not care as strongly about library service to youth as we do. But it is sometimes a stretch to master the new tasks required of us to manage youth services in our libraries, tasks often not significantly part of our formal education. So we look beyond our own departments for resources to help us. If we're especially lucky, we find a colleague to help us through the learning process, or better yet, a group of colleagues who have experienced similar situations and have succeeded or failed and learned from their failures. Often we wish we could take that group of mentors with us when we change jobs.

In this book you have that kind of mobile resource: thirteen experienced, candid professionals writing to share the how-to's—and sometimes the how-not-to's—of successfully managing youth services in public libraries. The first section of the book deals with general management issues. The State Library of Ohio's long-range planning expert Floyd C. Dickman opens the book with a chapter on the reasons and methods of long-range planning as it relates to youth services. Kathleen Deerr's excellent piece on budgets provides information on the various types as well as advice on preparation and winning support for your budget. A very successful grant writer herself, Sherry Des Enfants gives readers the why, what, who, where, and how of seeking alternative funding in her piece on grantsmanship. System youth services manager Gretchen Wronka and associate information management professor Mary M. Wagner did a survey of youth services coordinators throughout the country to gather information for their chapter on policies and procedures. The general management issues section ends with Virginia Walters's thorough chapter on the need for and mechanics of evaluation.

Section two, personnel issues, begins with the topic of job descriptions, illumined in useful detail by Yvette Johnson. In her chapter, Maria B. Salvadore explores the challenges of recruiting and retaining qualified youth services librarians and offers some innovative suggestions. Kathleen Staerkel tackles the relatively unexplored area of new staff orientation, and presents sensible suggestions as well as helpful checklists. Mary Fellows delves into the need for and methods of providing youth services staff with continuing education, and Marie C. Orlando discusses the philosophy and techniques of evaluating employees, proposing a step-by-step approach as well as sample evaluation forms.

In section three the issue under scrutiny is communication. Strategies and tips on conducting effective meetings are provided by Mary Fellows, followed by a practical discussion from Kathy Toon on developing and maintaining positive staff relations, no matter what the size of library. Concluding this section and the book is Melody Lloyd Allen's piece on the cooperation between agencies and the interpersonal networking that strengthens our service and enriches our professional and sometimes personal lives.

As is evident above, the issues this book covers comprise the foundation of youth services management today. Each author has written in her or his unique style a practical piece that will, we trust, in some way stimulate discussion or illumine a facet of youth services management. Taken as a whole, it is the editors' hope that this book will assist readers in becoming the new professional, well versed in management skills, whose efforts are crucial to the continued existence of quality service to youth in libraries.

MARY FELLOWS

Chapter 1

The Why and How of Planning

Floyd C. Dickman

Why Do We Have Planning?

Libraries have changed drastically in the last decades, particularly in youth services. Some of the changes can be attributed to the advancement of technology, a mobile population, and altering school curriculum. In the current economic situation librarians must take a critical look at existing services and the available resources. Any organization, in order to remain effective, must periodically review its performance and make improvements based on that review. Given the mission of public libraries and the changing conditions they face, this performance review is vital, not only for effective services but also for the continued existence of libraries. Youth services librarians must play an assertive and vital role in this review and in the resulting planning process.

Regardless of why libraries undertake to do planning, there are several reasons or benefits to do so. Among the major reasons are to

Establish priorities of service to all clientele, including youth

Make decisions based on fact and know what long-term consequences might be

Provide a vision for the future

Provide for a more effective and efficient organization, both internally among staff and externally within and beyond the community

Decrease frequency and nature of crises

Build staff teamwork and expertise

Planning can provide some or all of these benefits.

Background of Library Planning

While planning has been part of the human experience since time began, businessmen and librarians began to emphasize planning as a process in the late sixties. Since then the number of libraries using some type of planning process seems to be growing dramatically. Additionally, the publication of articles and books on the use of planning has grown steadily. These publications have been encouraged by the federal government, by state libraries, and by professional library organizations who have promoted the use of planning. As a result, many youth librarians are incorporating planning into their job descriptions.

Research has shown that those businesses or libraries that improve their performance have done so after engaging in a systematic planning process. Head librarians often use current statistical data about the community, involve a variety of persons in the planning process in order to develop a commitment to the planned improvements, and secure assistance from persons who can help them in specific planning and improvement tasks. Youth librarians must take part in the overall library planning process.

How Do We Organize the Planning Process?

The planning process consists of a number of major steps. Depending on the document you read, these can vary slightly. The best examples, containing a comprehensive description of these, can be found in *Planning and Role Setting for Public Libraries* by Charles R. McClure, et al. (1987) and in *A Planning Process for Public Libraries* by Vernon E. Palmour, et al. (1980). I highly recommend that these documents, published by the American Library Association, be examined closely. For the purpose of brevity, I have modified the planning process slightly to include the following steps:

Determine the role of the public library in the community

Evaluate current library services and resources

Assess community library needs

Set goals, objectives, and priorities

Develop strategies for change

Implement strategies

Monitor and evaluate progress toward goals and objectives

Revise periodically

Once the determination has been made to do planning for the library, a planning committee must be selected. This committee, ideally composed of people representing all aspects of the community, is a working group. It is suggested to keep it small enough to allow for individual input but also large enough to provide a wide range of interests. There needs to be a lot of interaction among the committee members. It is advisable to include people who have a strong commitment to a planning process.

The committee should represent larger groups in the community (businesses, schools, service organizations, etc.) as well as groups who have an interest in the library (the Friends of the Library, the board of trustees or other library policy makers). Committee composition should also have representatives from the library itself, including library administration, department or division heads, support staff, and any branches. This ensures that persons who are involved in providing important library services, such as youth services, reference, and so on, will not only have a say in determining the future of those services but they will also know what is currently happening with those services. Equally important as committee members are persons representing library users and nonusers. Try to keep the number of committee members below fifteen, however, as the group becomes too unwieldy beyond this number.

Determination of Roles

Libraries are encouraged to develop a mission statement that incorporates one or more roles as the first step in planning. A role, as defined in *A Planning Process for Public Libraries,* "should be concrete, stating who is to be served by specific services"[1] and should reflect the local library's assessment of its functions in the community. The role statements, when combined, become part of the mission statement, which will provide a focus for the library.

There are many considerations that need to be taken into account when determining these roles. Some of these are the service area of the library, the segments of the population served, the impact of other service agencies so materials and services are not duplicated, demographic trends, local economic conditions, and the growth or decrease in businesses.

There are at least two service role choices for youth services managers, taken from *Output Measures for Public Library Service to Children,* by Virginia A. Walter: "Preschoolers' Door to Learning" and "Formal Education Support Center." (While these roles relate directly to children, there are many other roles that the library can chose to serve its entire clientele.) Choosing the "Preschoolers' Door to Learning" role would focus on serving young children, parents and children together, or those persons who work directly with preschoolers in other agencies. Through these services libraries are trying to instill an interest in and a life-long love of reading and learning. Selecting "Formal Education Support Center" as a role would mean channeling resources to materials and services that would assist in formal course work and enhance individual learning.

While choosing among roles may be difficult, it is possible to focus on more than one. Whatever the combination of roles, it is hoped that they will lead children to become life-long readers and users of libraries.

Once developed, a library mission and role statement can and should be a guide to the development of all aspects of the library. A clear statement can be used to decide how money, staff, and time will be expended in the face of competing demands.

It is vital that everyone involved in the operation of the library, including the director, staff, and governing body, agree in principle on what the library is trying to provide and to whom. Libraries cannot afford to be unfocused when the results can cause confusion and contention.

Evaluation and Assessment of Services and Community

After determining the mission and role, it is time to evaluate the current services and resources. Determine early in the process just how much data you are going to collect. Know exactly the purpose of the data, then you will eliminate the collection of excess data which has no relevance to the research being done. No one has the time to collect unneeded information or to sort out what is important after volumes of data have been collected.

It is up to the planning committee to determine what data is needed. The necessary data usually falls into several categories. These would include management data (circulation figures, book turnover rate, program attendance, etc.), community profile (demographics, projected population growth rate, other information providers, etc.), citizen comments, and staff comments. *A Planning Process for Public Libraries* provides examples of surveys that can be used with these groups. It also breaks down the citizen group into specific categories.

After the surveys have been completed, the data must be tabulated and a report generated. It is usually best if one person is responsible for the tabulating of the data and the writing of the report.

Another valuable tool to use in completing these assessment tasks is *Evaluation Strategies and Techniques for Public Library Children's Services* by Jane Robbins, et al. The authors of this book have provided an outstanding tool that not only provides excellent directions and background of evaluation techniques but also includes many charts and forms that will prove to be helpful in gathering the data that is needed to assess library services and community needs. Some of the materials in the Robbins book have been adapted specifically to use in children's services from *Output Measures for Public Libraries,* published by the American Library Association. Virginia A. Walter's book *Output Measures for Public Library Service to Children* also provides a wealth of information on how to proceed with assessment of services specifically for children. The practical advice is extremely valuable in carrying out the statistical data-gathering process.

After the data have been collected, the next step is to assess what the community needs from its library. It is important for the planning committee to read carefully the final reports for all the data generated. In this way the planning committee will have an understanding of the services that are important to the library community and will be better prepared to write goals for the future.

Setting and Writing Goals and Objectives

The writing of goals and objectives does not occur in a vacuum but utilizes all the information gathered in the evaluation of services and community needs. While goals and objectives are written to address the total library operation, they must take into consideration such factors as the social, political, and economic environments as well as available staff and funds, limitations imposed by the facility, and the availability of other library services in the area.

Goals are broad statements of desired ends to which the library is striving. Because goals are stated in broad terms (ideals) they are not measurable. Goals suggest the future direction that the library wishes to take. It is absolutely necessary that these goals be compatible with and supportive of the roles the library has selected. Examples of goals for children's services include "to improve the effectiveness of children's services" and "to provide library materials better suited to the needs and interest of preschoolers."

Once the goals have been determined, it is time to select and write the objectives to carry out each goal. It is important that objectives contain some action for future improvement of services or movement in a new direction. Objectives need to be specific enough so that a library staff member or library department can be assigned responsibility for achieving a particular objective.

Charles McClure suggests seven criteria for judging the validity of an objective.

Is it, generally speaking, a call to action?

Does it suggest courses of action?

Is it explicit enough to suggest concrete actions?

Can it be measured?

Is it time limited?

Is it ambitious enough to be challenging?

Does it support both the library's goal and role statement?

An objective to go with the goal of better preschool service would be "to increase the number of materials purchased for preschoolers in 1994 by 15 percent by December 31, 1995."

As the planning committee develops objectives, many statements of achievement will be generated. While this is predictable, we also know that not all objectives can be achieved equally. Therefore the planning committee must rank their objectives in a priority order, usually from most important to least important. This ranking should occur only after all the objectives to achieve a certain goal are written, and should include all objectives generated.

While all objectives are important, their priority will increase or decrease with the availability of funding needed to carry them out. The ranking should be done using three fiscal projections: (1) less funding for the library, (2) no increase in funding except for inflation (status quo), and (3) increased funding. The committee will also need to look at the objectives to determine into what categories they fall: essential objectives, important objectives, and desirable objectives. By ranking in this way you will end up with three very different lists of objectives.

	Less Funding	Status Quo	Increased Funding
Essential	A	A	A
		B	B
			C
Important	B	C	D
	C	D	E
	D	E	F
Desirable	E	F	
	F		

FIGURE 1.   Library Objectives

   Figure 1 demonstrates how the completed objectives will appear. Each letter represents a specific objective, whose ranking as essential, important, or desirable changes with the financial climate.

Development and Implementation of Strategies

   Once the goals and objectives have been confirmed and the objectives have been ranked in priority order, the next step in the planning process is to develop the strategies that will be used to implement the objectives. As defined in *A Planning Process for Public Libraries,* strategies are "a set of options or methods for improving library service." Strategies are also referred to as activities in that they specify the tasks that must be accomplished in order to achieve an objective. Hereafter, the term activity will be used instead of strategy because it more accurately denotes action and progress.

   Many activities should be generated for each objective. The generation of activities needs to be done by members of the planning committee and those persons who will be responsible for executing the activities. Therefore, if the objective falls under the role of Preschoolers' Door to Learning, the head of youth services and the youth services staff should be included in the process. This process should include brainstorming sessions in order to develop all possible activities for an objective. Creativity and innovation should be strongly encouraged. No idea should be discarded or restricted in the first round of these sessions solely because it is not immediately possible to do the activity.

   The generation of activities is the most creative step of the planning process. During the process the planning committee is required to reexamine the library's traditional services and operations and devise new ones that may more effectively meet its ends. The activities have to be compared and evaluated in terms of their effectiveness in attaining the library's objectives, the relative cost in achieving them, and the priorities given to the many objectives that the library is trying to achieve. The result of the development of the activities should be library services that meet the needs of the community.

Once the activities have been chosen, specific plans must be made to carry them out. It must be determined who is to perform the activity, when, and how. This information is included in the long-range plan. Using the role Preschoolers' Door to Learning and the objective "To increase the number of materials purchased for preschoolers by 15 percent by December 31, 1995," an appropriate activity would be "Each staff member in Youth Services will spend two hours per week reviewing professional journals in order to find materials suggested for use with preschoolers."

Evaluation and Revision

Implementation of activities does not ensure the success of a long-range plan. Remember to keep in mind that achievement of the objective is the purpose of activities, and therefore activities may need to be adjusted or refocused to successfully attain your goal. With this in mind, it is necessary to plan for a formal evaluation procedure not only for the measurement of the activities but for the entire long-range planning process. Use of the Activity Responsibility Chart (figure 2) is recommended to assist in this two-phased evaluation procedure. The chart is adaptable; it can be used for evaluating a single activity or serve as the basis of evaluation of the entire long-range plan.

Usually the planning committee is responsible for developing and conducting the overall evaluation, but those persons who are responsible for the day-to-day implementation of activities must also be involved, as they can provide timely and relevant information. For this reason it is necessary for each staff member to be committed to the long-range plan, and to be involved in tracking the accomplishment of the activities for which he or she is responsible. The activity responsibility charts allow various chains of related goals, objectives, and activities to be displayed for each staff or department. They will provide a view of how each activity

Person Responsible:

Goal Number: Planning Area:

Objective Number:

Activity Number:

	Date Started		Date Completed	
Steps in implementation	Planned	Actual	Planned	Actual

FIGURE 2. Activity Responsibility Chart

relates to the library's total plan, thereby giving a sense of purpose. The progress made can also be executed without confusion and redundant action. By examining all of the charts, the planning committee will have an overview of the entire plan's implementation and its progress.

Keeping a record of the planned and actual starting and completion dates of each activity can be a valuable tool in measuring progress. This task will also help focus attention on the many variables that arise during a plan's implementation. It will also provide clues that will help in determining why certain activities did not take place as planned. It is extremely important in carrying out a plan that all staff members interact and coordinate their respective activities. If this is not done it may result in having a number of items not undertaken or completed. It is important to remember that the success of an individual activity is not more important than the total operation of the library. Care must be taken to prevent conflict and competition among the library departments, programs, and individual staff members. To ensure progress in completing an activity, the responsible person should make notations on the accomplishment about midway between the starting and ending date. Individuals should refer to the activity charts on a regular basis.

The person who is responsible for an activity should complete the chart as soon as the activity is accomplished. Personal observations as to why an activity succeeded or failed must be documented immediately. This information will be extremely important to the planning committee as the members evaluate the current long-range plan and rewrite it for the future. Communication must be open between the persons responsible for activities and the planning committee so that feedback is generated as soon as possible. This is vital because much of the time there are activities that heavily affect other services or activities in the library.

If activities create conflicts, it will be necessary for the planning committee to modify the plan. This is another reason for communication to be open and ongoing. Adjustments must be made to ensure that the plan is proceeding efficiently and effectively.

Once a year the planning committee must consider an evaluation of the entire plan. Some questions that can be used are:

Has the plan demonstrated that the chosen roles for the library are appropriate?

Has the plan been a success or a failure?

Have changes occurred in the community or in the library?

Have any unforeseen opportunities or problems arisen?

What has been the library's performance during the past year?

When the overall evaluation is complete it is suggested that a report or chart of the accomplishments and future tasks be prepared. This document can be distributed to staff and to the public at large. In this way recognition is given to the people who have done the work, and the document also serves as a valuable tool in maintaining enthusiasm for planning.

Conclusion

Planning is a valuable tool that allows us to organize for the future, both on a short-term and a long-term basis. While the basic steps have been outlined for persons who are interested, it is important to keep in mind that planning is not a one-time activity. Rather it is a continuous process that involves people who serve and are served. Communication must be maintained at all levels in order to ensure that the plan is successful. As a library finishes the primary cycle of planning, it must establish a secondary cycle. Each successive completed plan must be evaluated and further developed in order to be of any value as a working document. Planning will be successful only if it is undertaken by people who are flexible and service oriented.

Note   1. Vernon E. Palmour, Marcia C. Bellassai, and Nancy V. DeWath, *A Planning Process for Public Libraries* (Chicago: American Library Association, 1980), 55.

Bibliography

Altman, Ellen, Ernest R. DeProspo, Philip M. Clark, and Ellen Connor Clark. *A Data Gathering and Instruction Manual for Performance Measures in Public Libraries.* Chicago: Celadon Press, 1976.

Anthony, William P. *Practical Strategic Planning: A Guide and Manual for Line Managers.* Westport, Conn.: Greenwood Press, 1985.

Bolt, Nancy and Corinne Johnson. *Options for Small Public Libraries in Massachusetts: Recommendations and a Planning Guide.* Chicago: American Library Association, 1985.

Carter, Jane Robbins. "Whatever Shall We Do? Standards for Public Library Service." In *Public Librarianship: A Reader,* by J. R. Carter, 137–42. Littleton, Colo.: Libraries Unlimited, 1982.

Davis, Peter. "Libraries at the Turning Point: Issues in Proactive Planning." In *The Management Process: A Selection of Readings for Librarians,* ed. Ruth J. Person. Chicago: American Library Association, 1983.

DeProspo, Ernest R., Ellen Altman, and Kenneth Beasley. *Performance Measures for Public Libraries.* Chicago: American Library Association, 1973.

Detweiler, Mary Jo. "Planning More Than Process." *Library Journal* 108 (January 1, 1983):23–26.

Foundations of Quality: Guidelines for Public Library Service to Children. Chicago: American Library Association, 1981.

Gault, R. R. "Planning for Children's Services in Public Libraries." *Public Libraries* 25 (Summer 1986):60–62.

Hawgood, John. "You Too Can Be a Library Planner Part I." *Public Libraries* (Spring 1981):19–22. "Part II." (Summer 1981):53–56.

Jackson, Inez L. and E. Ramsey. *Library Planning and Budgeting.* New York: Franklin Watts, 1986.

Koening, M. E. D. and L. Kerson. "Strategic and Long Range Planning in Library and Information Centers." In *Advances in Library Administration and Organi-*

zation, Vol. 2. Greenwich, Conn.: JAI Press, 1983. This article is a primer and literature review.

Lynch, Mary Jo. "Measurement of Public Library Activity: The Search for Practical Methods." *Wilson Library Bulletin* 57, no. 5 (January 1983):388–93.

Manion, E. S. "The Planning Process." *Bookmark* 43 (Winter 1985):94–96. This article presents the planning process from a trustee's point of view.

Mason, Richard O. and E. Burton Swanson. *Measurement for Management Decision.* Reading, Mass.: Addison-Wesley, 1981.

McClure, Charles R. "Library Planning: A Status Report." In *The ALA Yearbook of Library and Information Services,* 7–16. Chicago: American Library Association, 1986.

McClure, Charles R. "Planning for Library Services: Lessons and Opportunities." *Journal of Library Administration* 2, nos. 2/3/4 (1981):7–28.

McClure, Charles R. "The Planning Process: Strategies for Action." In *Strategies for Action, Strategies for Library Administration: Concepts and Approaches,* ed. Charles R. McClure and Alan R. Samuels. Littleton, Colo.: Libraries Unlimited, 1982.

McClure, Charles R., Douglas L. Zweizig, Nancy A. Van House, and Mary Jo Lynch. "Output Measures: Myths, Realities, and Prospects." *Public Libraries* 25 (Summer 1986):49–52.

McClure, Charles R., Amy Owen, Douglas L. Zweizig, Mary Jo Lynch, and Nancy A. Van House. *Planning and Role Setting for Public Libraries: A Manual of Options and Procedures.* Chicago: American Library Association, 1987.

Palmour, Vernon E., Marcia C. Bellassai, and Nancy V. DeWath. *A Planning Process for Public Libraries.* Chicago: American Library Association, 1980.

Riggs, Donald E. *Strategic Planning for Library Managers.* Phoenix, Ariz.: Oryx Press, 1984.

Robbins, Jane, Holly Willett, Mary Jane Wiseman, and Douglas L. Zweizig. *Evaluation Strategies and Techniques for Public Library Children's Services: A Sourcebook.* Madison: Univ. of Wisconsin, School of Library and Information Studies, 1990.

Sager, D. J. "Planning Factors in Large and Small Public Libraries." *Public Libraries* 25 (Spring 1986):26–29.

Sertic, Kenneth J. "Rural Public Libraries and the Planning Process." *Public Libraries* (Spring 1982):19–20.

Shearer, Kenneth. "PLA's Seminar on A Planning Process for Public Libraries." *Public Libraries* (Winter 1979):98–100.

Speer, Rick. "Guidelines for Preplanning." *Public Libraries* (Spring 1983): 26–27.

Van House, Nancy A., Mary Jo Lynch, Charles R. McClure, Douglas L. Zweizig, and Eleanor Jo Rodger. *Output Measures for Public Libraries: A Manual of Standardized Procedures,* 2d ed. Chicago: American Library Association, 1987.

Walter, Virginia A. *Output Measures for Public Library Service to Children: A Manual of Standardized Procedures.* Chicago: American Library Association, 1992.

Zweizig, Douglas L. "Tailoring Measures to Fit Your Service: A Guide for the Manager of Reference Services." *Reference Librarian,* no. 11 (Fall-Winter 1984): 53–61.

Chapter 2

Budgeting

Kathleen Deerr

Budget—the word can evoke a vast array of meanings and feelings: restrictions, balancing, accountability, record keeping, justifying. Staying within a budget, whether it be personal or business, is rarely pleasant, but rather all too often, a difficult chore. So why do we do it? Let's stop for a moment and examine what our lives would be like without budgets.

To illustrate this, just imagine shopping for your weekly supply of food but having no idea how much money you have to spend. You might fill up your shopping cart with everything needed for the week, and when you get to the checkout, place the items on the counter in no particular order. The cashier starts to ring up the items and about halfway through informs you that you are out of funds. You return home with oatmeal, cookies, macaroni, fruit, and dishwashing detergent. Not exactly the ingredients of a well-stocked kitchen!

While this scenario may seem absurd, it is unfortunately not that different from the way in which many youth services librarians are expected (or choose) to run their libraries or departments. Just as the shopper was unable to attain a goal of providing a week's worth of well-balanced nutritional food, librarians cannot possibly meet the goals of their departments and contribute to the larger goals of their public library or school without a budget.

Let us get back to our shopper. The following week she returns to the supermarket with the same goal but this time knowing what her budget is. She has also carefully assessed her current supplies (there are still plenty of cookies), knows how many people she is trying to feed, and has developed menus for seven breakfasts, lunches, and dinners. I am sure her shopping cart will look quite different from the week before. Of course, to stay within her budget, priorities had to be established (since nutrition was important, milk would be purchased before ice cream), meals had to be planned, and choices had to be made. Having filet mignon for one dinner would necessitate the other meals be very inexpensive. Perhaps sticking to all mid-priced meals would be best. If there were money remaining for ice cream, would it be the rocky road or cherry vanilla? These are indeed tough choices, but the shopper knows what they are and knows the goal of providing nutritional food is being met despite the fact that she cannot purchase everything everyone wants.

When looking at a budget in this light, it reveals itself to be a necessary and extremely useful tool. Budgets have been described by experts as "a series of goals with price tags attached . . . a mechanism for making choices among alternative expenditures."[1] A budget indicates the resources that will be needed to meet goals and objectives within a prescribed period of time.[2] Since most youth services libraries are parts of larger institutions, budgets can also serve as a scale of weights and measures comparing the youth services library budget with those of other departments within the institution. How this is done, of course, is determined by the goals, objectives, and priorities of each institution. If, for instance, important determining factors in departmental budget allocations were the population served and the circulation, and youth services accounted for 30 percent of the population and 50 percent of the circulation, one would expect the department to receive at least 30 percent of the total public service department budget. When making these comparisons, be sure to compare only similar departments. It would not be valid to compare the youth services budget with that of technical services.

While the last ten years have seen great accomplishments in standards and guidelines for youth services, a survey of the literature does not reveal any formula or specific guidelines for youth services department budgets in regard to a total library budget. The 1984 Standards for Youth Services in Public Libraries of New York State mentions, "Approximately thirty percent of the library materials budget should be spent for children's materials."[3] The document further indicates how this money should be divided among the various types of materials, but gives no objective rationale to support these numbers. *Information Power: Guidelines for School Library Media Programs* does provide formulas for materials and equipment budgets.[4]

Having a budget for a school or youth services department in a public library forces the librarian to assess the current state of the department and the population it serves, evaluate departmental goals and objectives, plan for future goals and objectives, prioritize objectives, and compare departmental allocations with similar departments. It also provides another very important element—clear, direct communication between you and your administration. This is a vital factor in developing and maintaining a strong department.

Types of Budgets

The budget format you develop and present will most likely be determined by that used by your administration. While there are many types of budgets, the three major types most often used by libraries are (1) line-item, (2) planning-programming, and (3) zero-based.[5]

Line-Item Budget

This format has been widely used for many years. Each major area of spending is assigned a code: personnel, materials, programs, equipment, conference and travel, etc. Each code becomes a line-item in the budget. Traditionally this involves three basic steps: (1) last year's spending for each code is given, (2) last year's funding is incremented for increased costs within each code, (3) additional costs for new projects, programs, materials, etc., further increases those item codes.[6] If an increase in a code is requested beyond the usual inflation rate or if a decrease occurs, a brief explanation is provided (*see* table 1).

TABLE 1.   Children's and Parents' Services Department (CPSD) Budget Program

Code	Explanation	1991–92	1992–93
141C	Professional	239,510	255,147
	5 Full Time	192,510	198,522
	New Full Time		26,533 [1]
	Part-time Hours	47,000	30,092 [2]
142C	Clerical	49,210	54,678 [3]
143C	Pages	64,400	71,000 [4]
410C	Books	92,000	98,000 [5]
412C	Recordings	6,300	6,600
413C	Serials and Periodicals	8,400	8,800
415C	AV/Filmstrip Materials	2,100	1,100 [6]
417C	Video Cassettes	19,500	20,500
419C	Computer Software	3,400	4,000 [7]
429C	Realia	2,800	3,940 [8]
430C	Office and Library Supplies	16,000	16,800
434C	Printing	3,800	4,400
435C	Continuing Ed., Conference and Travel	3,200	3,200
437C	Programs	17,600	19,800
	TOTALS	$528,220	$567,965

1. These 35 hours are being taken from part-time hours already in the budget.
2. This is a 7% increase in part-time librarian hours remaining after 35 hours were transferred to full time. Total library circulation increased 10%. CPSD increased 14%. This accounts for 53% of total circulation. Reference queries increased by 11%.
3. The senior clerk test is scheduled for spring. I anticipate recommending three employees for senior clerk positions starting in December. This reflects 6 months of clerical salaries plus 6 months of senior clerk salaries.
4. This 10% increase is to keep up with the 14% increase in CPSD circulation.
5. This increase is to cover: (a) inflation 5% and (b) the purchase of book materials on CD-ROM, which would save space and provide greater access for patrons.
6. $1,000 of this money will be transferred to 429.
7. This will keep up with 5% inflation plus give us funds to purchase some networkable software for staff use.
8. Provide a 5% increase for puzzles, puppets, and Parent/Toddler materials. It also includes $1,000 transferred from 415C to build the Nintendo collection (90% of our suggestions requested Nintendos).

One advantage of this model is that it can be used to monitor expenses over two or three years (depending on how many years' budgets are included in each year's proposal).[7] Furthermore, line-item budgets are simple to construct, easy to compute, and each item is clearly defined, necessitating only minimal explanation. Critics of this type of budget point to the fact that it does not stress library service to the public.[8] Since goals and objectives are not integrated with various item codes, it is a poor planning tool, and cuts can be made without making a conscious connection to specific services.[9]

However, by adapting and elaborating on the traditional line-item budget, the above-mentioned disadvantages are not a problem. For instance, under the program line of a departmental line-item budget proposal, one can easily include many subcategories that clearly indicate what each program will cost. Your administration can see exactly where the money will be spent and identify which programs will be eliminated if this area of the budget is cut (*see* table 2). While the total library budget request will probably not include every bit of information covered in a departmental request, those areas that the administration feels may be most scrutinized and subject to cuts can be presented in more detail than others.

The line-item budget works especially well in an institution in which there are only three layers between the youth services department and the funding: the director, the board of trustees or other governing body, and the tax payers who vote directly on the budget. If a library is part of a large system with many layers, or is not funded directly by a public vote but instead receives monies from city or county funds, this type of budget may not work as well.

TABLE 2.   Line-Item Budget Showing Subcategories of Programs

Code	Explanation	1992–93	1993–94
437	Programs	17,600	19,200
	Summer Programs	6,000	6,300 [1]
	Summer Reading Clubs	4,000	4,200
	Young Teen Programs	500	800 [2]
	Parent/Toddler Workshops	2,600	3,200 [3]
	Holiday/School Break Programs	3,500	3,700
	Parents as Reading Partners	1,000	1,000

1. An additional sign language series ($300) will accommodate 50% of the 60 people on the waiting list.
2. Young teen library use has increased 40% since last year mainly because of the input of the Young Teen Advisory Board. We need to provide programs and activities that will maintain their interests.
3. This will allow 2 more sessions of Parent/Toddler Workshop, which will enable interested families to attend once per year. We now have 100 families on a waiting list.

Planning-Programming Budget

This budget is developed around the goals and objectives of a particular department or library for a specified period of time and emphasizes the output of services to the particular client group. Statements regarding the consequences of not funding a particular request and suggestions of an alternative program that can meet the objectives are usually included. Variations of this model may also include evaluation, making this a valuable planning tool. Programs can be defined by the functions the library staff performs, by the clientele served, or by service areas (book-mobiles, early childhood rooms, etc.). Libraries and departments usually determine their own program components.[10] As defined by Barry Devlin in his chapter "Basic Budget Primer: Choosing the Best Budget for Your Library," the steps involved for this type of budget might include (1) Defining the program objectives, (2) Delineating the major activities necessary to accomplish these objectives, (3) Determining the nature and level of resources needed to support the activities, (4) Developing the budget requirements, (5) Stating the requirements for all programs within your department using the above four steps.[11] One of the advantages of this type of budget is that it provides information on the actual cost of fulfilling each objective. It also outlines a detailed plan of action by which each objective will be fulfilled and often provides an evaluation mechanism. A disadvantage is that it is extremely labor intensive. In addition, financial responsibility for programs that span more than one department is difficult to determine. And if goals and objectives are not clearly defined, the result is a vague, unclear budget.[12] (A complete multipage example of this type of budget can be found in Mae Benne's *Principles of Children's Services in Public Libraries,* pp. 266–72.)

One example of planning-programming budgets is government grant proposals. While this method is certainly a wonderful planning, organizational, and evaluational tool, it is questionable whether it is worth the time and labor that would be necessary to develop an entire departmental budget in this manner. A combination of line-item and planning-program budget types might provide some of these advantages without the intensive labor input.

Zero-Based Budget

This model starts each year at a zero base rather than with what was allocated the year before. The budget is constructed through a complex process that examines every aspect of library service. Each unit or "decision package," as they are called, included in the budget must be justified every year. Costs of activities for each decision package are computed, prioritized, and ranked.[13] Advocates of this model point to the fact that since nothing is ever a given, and everything is so finely prioritized, this is the best method to determine the finest service for the least funding. Critics point to the fact that the benefits of ranking are more than set off by the amount of work needed to identify and justify each activity as well as the time spent documenting and prioritizing programs. (An example of a zero-based budget can be found in *The Bottom Line Reader: A Financial Handbook for Librarians,* p. 34.)

No matter what budget form is ultimately used, the goal is to present a document that is clear and informative, objectively supports your requests, and arms your administrator with facts and information necessary to justify and fight for your needs.

Budget Preparation

Depending on the structure of your institution, the head of youth services may or may not be included in the formal budget process. If you are not included, prepare your budget proposal anyway. Do not sit back like the victim who has no control and must simply take what is given. Then, staying within the hierarchy of your institution, meet with your supervisor (hopefully, part of the budget team), to present and justify your requests. While you will not get everything you request, this can establish the groundwork for future requests. If nothing else, it will certainly prove you are not just a nice person who loves books and children and thinks youth services should be funded just because everyone knows its wonderful benefits. As we all know, this type of thinking does not result in funding. Even if only one part of your request makes it into the final budget, it is a start.

Whether or not you are part of the formal budget team, make sure you include the youth services staff in at least the preliminary process. Everyone has a stake in his or her portion of the budget. As supervisor, you may ultimately determine the goals and objectives of youth services (always making sure they promote the overall goals and objectives of the total library) and their order of priority. But unless you are a one-person department, your colleagues must share your philosophy and feel part of the process. Having input into the budget certainly helps accomplish this.

In larger divisions this becomes even more critical. As departments grow, more and more duties are delegated, and the supervisor may no longer be the "expert" in a particular area (technology, for instance) and must rely on staff input regarding projected needs, costs, and information. If this is the case, each person responsible for a particular area can formally or informally submit his or her budgetary requests. The manager can then meet with each staff member individually and finally with the group as a whole to develop priorities in relation to long- and short-term goals of youth services and the library. Just as your division will rarely get everything requested, neither will individual staff members. It is important that they see the "big picture" so they can understand the reasons why their requests were not funded.

While formal budget preparation may involve only a few months, budget preparation is an ongoing activity. Keep a "next fiscal year" folder for ideas, suggestions, etc. This includes all areas of the budget: personnel, materials, equipment, programs, and conference and travel. Make notes on equipment prices, changes in usage, demographics of the community, collection wear and tear, availability of new materials in new formats, the need for additional collections, possible upcoming raises and promotions of staff, etc. Where necessary, keep statistics that can help justify requests. Some of these statistics can be obtained by using *Output Measures for Public Library Service to Children.*

When the time comes to start the actual budget procedure (usually six to seven months before the start of the next fiscal year), it is helpful if you have a direct line of communication with your administrator. It can save you a lot of work and time if you know what the broad budgetary picture will be. If this is the year the administration is trying to obtain sizable raises for the staff or if benefit premiums just tripled, this is probably not the year to propose significant increases in other areas. If, on the other hand, the board of trustees and administration have decided family literacy will be top priority, you can relate most of your increases to that topic.

Budget proposals can be shaped from the bottom up or from the top down. In good financial times, they usually develop from the bottom up. This is always preferable since you can slowly but steadily build in increased funding each year to support additional short-term objectives that will meet long-term goals. The other method almost always involves holding the fiscal line or cutting back, which is more challenging but certainly not as much fun.

Whatever direction is taken and whatever budget type is used, brush up on your math and pay attention to details. If you have full-time personnel who will receive a salary increase three months into the new fiscal year, you need to calculate three months of the salary at the current rate and nine months of the salary at the increased rate. When requesting new equipment or maintenance contracts on older equipment, get quotes in writing. Always check at least three vendors so you can prove you are getting a competitive price.

Most budget proposals are based on or at least compared with that of the previous year. Any changes, increases, decreases, or transfers of monies need to be documented and explained in objective measurable terms. When looking for an increase in librarian hours, it is not enough to state that youth services is so busy the librarians never sit down, children are waiting four deep at the reference desk, and you are three months behind in your selection journals. While all this may be true, it sounds like a subjective complaint. (Inevitably your director or trustee will walk into the department during the one afternoon when the whole town is at sports tryouts and he or she will not understand why you need more help!) Proudly and objectively stating (from annual statistics) that reference questions increased by 20 percent, summer reading club enrollment went up by 30 percent, youth services accounted for 53 percent of the total annual library circulation, and the number of class visits doubled has much more impact.

Following is a personal experience that may be read as a case study illustrating the value of statistics in justifying budget requests. My first experience with statistics and budgets actually came before I was responsible for developing and maintaining a departmental budget. I was a young, energetic librarian at a brand new library and the only staff member in youth services. The first summer the library was open to the public we registered 553 children for the summer reading club. The second summer we registered 979. I kept asking for more help and finally got a part-time page for the summer. At the end of the second summer I sent a survey to ten of the busiest youth services departments in Suffolk County asking how many children enrolled in and completed the reading club and how many youth services librarians, clerks, and pages were in the department. The results were incredible. The Mastics-Moriches-Shirley Community Library had the third highest enrollment and the fewest staff of the ten (much larger at the time) libraries that responded. I shared this information with my director and was invited to a meeting to share this with the trustees. The trustees were so astounded that they approved a half-time youth services librarian position to start immediately.

Understandably such positive results made me a little statistics crazy until I learned the golden rule of statistics—just because it can be measured does not mean you should measure it. Look at what needs to be justified and determine what statistics and output measures can help do so. Certain things may be counted every year (reference questions, circulation, class visits), while others may come and go as needed. Once you establish a clear pattern that school visits increase summer program enrollment, it is no longer necessary to document it every year.

Accountability of past allocations can also add credence to increased requests. When public service computers were introduced to the children's department, the response was so overwhelming there was little opposition to adding an additional computer and software every year until we could meet the demand.

It is very important to maintain the current year's budget. Keeping track of a departmental budget can be accomplished in a variety of ways, from the department head doing the bookkeeping, to reports generated by any one or combination of the department, technical services, personnel, or administration. Knowing where you stand financially at any given time during the year is vital. A vast array of computer programs and spread sheets make this job much less cumbersome and time consuming than it was in the past. While it may still be tempting to let accounting or administration oversee the department budget, if you want to keep control of your department's money, you have to accept this responsibility.

Winning Support and Influence

If you have done your homework, kept your statistics, and put together a clear, well-organized, objective budget request, you may think it's now out of your hands. However, just as plants tend to grow better in cultivated soil, budget requests also fare better if a little time is spent "cultivating" the decision makers. This goes beyond mere communication and enters into the art of public relations. Just exactly who your "public" is depends upon the structure and funding source of your particular library. Once you have defined who these people are, think about how you can positively influence them.

Before going any further, a word of caution is needed. Each administrator has his or her own style and protocol in dealing with boards of trustees, funding sources, patrons, and other decision makers. Make sure everything you do has the full blessing of your administration. There is no better way to negatively influence administrators than by doing something behind their backs or going over their heads.

Once you have determined what your boundaries are with the various key players, keep in mind that just as budgeting is an ongoing process, positively influencing and gaining the support of people in key areas must also be ongoing if it is to be effective. For instance, you may wish to attend (with the director's permission) two or three board of trustee meetings per year to keep trustees informed of new activities, special projects, and the state of the department in general. If the structure of your institution does not allow for this, you may still reach these people while addressing other organizations, such as civic, school, and religious groups. Take every opportunity to get out into your community and let the public know what your department has to offer and its many successes. Listen to their comments and ask them what they want. When a trustee hears three hundred parents state that the quality of children's programming is wonderful, but the quantity is insufficient, it has more impact than anything you can present. Invite trustees to participate in some of your programs: handing out reading club certificates, judging a talent contest, reading their favorite book during National Library Week. Then take these opportunities to casually share the costs and benefits of such programs. You might occasionally include information on patron needs that are not yet being fully addressed and share your vision on how that might be accomplished in the future. There are many subtle ways to involve trustees and keep them informed, and this can be very helpful at budget time.

These same concepts also apply to your administrator. Keep in mind though that while youth services is your whole world, it is just one (very important) piece of his or hers. So while you want to communicate, communicate, and communicate, keep it brief and, if possible, translate your information into administrative language: cost per patron, impact on circulation, increased patron satisfaction, contribution to long-term goals, etc. Share pertinent articles with him or her but highlight salient points. Mention a (your) new idea in passing and casually bring it up from time to time before making a formal request that requires funding. Do not forget, however, that administrators are human too, and they may get tired of dealing with all the complaints, problems, and statistics. Take advantage of situations that arise (waiting for the elevator), to share your human interest success stories, such as the one about the child who won the reading club party raffle. (He is the son of the president of the board of education and thought this was the best reading club ever.) Then mention how the additional funding for raffle prizes paid off both in enrollment and public relations. Casually presenting how specific activities in the youth services department increase library usage, patron satisfaction, and build public relations always pays off. Just remember not to inundate your administrator. No one wants to be constantly barraged (not even with positive information).

A brief word about colleagues is necessary here. Be aware that almost everything one department does affects others in some way. Communicate your ideas and plans with your colleagues, discuss the impact these might have on their departments, and build interdepartmental teamwork. This will help gain support for your programs and services instead of animosity. At funding time you want your administrator to remember your new program as a cost-effective literacy enhancer rather than the one that caused chaos at the circulation desk all summer, angering patrons and staff.

Finally, there are our patrons—the end users—the most important piece of the dynamic and the reason for our professional existence. Talk with them, listen to them, and do everything within your power and budget to meet their needs, for they are your strongest, most powerful allies and supporters. If your institution is funded by citizens voting directly for or against a proposed library budget, this is even more the case. Think of each and every one of your patrons as your ally; even the disgruntled, complaining ones can be an asset. The following two case studies illustrate this point.

There was a mother who constantly complained that we did not have enough programs for her children. When my director and I were unable to rectify matters to her satisfaction, she threatened to go to the board of trustees. Instead of getting defensive, my response was positive and encouraging. I explained that the more the community parents made their wishes known to the trustees, the easier it would be for me to get additional funding for children's and parents' services. When budget time came, that was exactly what happened.

Offering a "pilot project" of a new program or service can also be beneficial. Funding for our parent/toddler workshops was a result of such a pilot project. We had just moved into our permanent building and had the space but neither the staff nor program money needed to offer the workshops on a regular basis. With my director's approval, I overextended myself and offered a six-week pilot project serving fifty families. The response was so overwhelming we had 150 additional families on an interest list. Monies to fund the program were included in the next year's budget. The budget passed by more than three to one, and we had never seen so many mothers with toddlers in strollers come into the library to vote! If your patrons do not vote directly on your budget, the process is certainly not as simple, but it can still work. Your patrons are more than likely also the constituents of those determining your budget. They could write letters, attend meetings, or hold rallies. Many a branch library has survived or had hours restored in response to patron protests.

Youth services librarians are notoriously dedicated, hard-working individuals always willing to take that extra step to serve their patrons. Some even go so far as to refer to their work as a calling rather than a profession. If we are truly committed to providing the best library services possible, we, like our fictitious shopper, need to acknowledge the importance of the entire budget process and work to become active participants within that process.

Notes   1. Aaron Wildavsky, *The New Politics of the Budgetary Process* (Glenview, Ill.: Scott, Foresman, 1988), 2.

2. Adele M. Fasick, *Managing Children's Services in the Public Library* (Englewood, Colo.: Libraries Unlimited, 1991), 103.

3. Task Force on Standards for Youth Services, Youth Services Section, NYLA, *Standards for Youth Services in Public Libraries of New York State* (New York: New York Library Association, 1984), 4.

4. American Association of School Librarians and Association for Educational Communications and Technology, *Information Power: Guidelines for School Library Media Programs* (Chicago: American Library Association, 1988), 124–30.

5. Mae Benne, *Principles of Children's Services in Public Libraries* (Chicago: American Library Association, 1991), 60.

6. *The Bottom Line Reader: A Financial Handbook for Librarians* (New York: Neal-Schuman, 1990), 31.

7. Benne, *Principles,* 61.

8. *Bottom Line Reader,* 32.

9. Benne, *Principles,* 61.

10. Ibid., 61, 62.

11. *Bottom Line Reader,* 33.

12. *Bottom Line Reader,* 34.

13. Benne, *Principles,* 63, 64.

Bibliography

American Association of School Librarians and Association for Educational Communications and Technology. *Information Power: Guidelines for School Library Media Programs.* Chicago: American Library Association, 1988.

Benne, Mae. *Principles of Children's Services in Public Libraries.* Chicago: American Library Association, 1991.

Bottom Line Reader: A Financial Handbook for Librarians. Edited by Betty-Carol Sellen and Betty J. Turock. New York: Neal-Schuman, 1990.

Fasick, Adele M. *Managing Children's Services in the Public Library.* Englewood, Colo.: Libraries Unlimited, 1991.

Task Force on Standards for Youth Services, Youth Services Section, NYLA. *Standards for Youth Services in Public Libraries of New York State.* New York: New York Library Association, 1984.

Walter, Virginia A. *Output Measures for Public Library Service to Children.* Chicago: American Library Association, 1992.

Wildavsky, Aaron. *The New Politics of the Budgetary Process.* Glenview, Ill.: Scott, Foresman, 1988.

For Further Reading

Reader in Library Administration. Edited by Paul Wasserman and Mary Lee Bundy. Englewood, Colo.: Information Handling Services, Library and Education Div., 1968.

Rollock, Barbara, T. *Public Library Services for Children.* Hamden, Conn.: Shoe String, 1988.

Turock, Betty J. and Andra Pedolsky. *Creating a Financial Plan: A How-to-Do-It Manual for Librarians.* New York: Neal-Schuman, 1992.

Chapter 3

Seeking Alternative Funding: Grantsmanship

Sherry Des Enfants

Why Pursue Grants?

If there are services or materials which your library should offer to children in your community but can't afford, it may be time to consider writing a grant. As a youth services manager, you have an obligation to remain aware of and responsive to the changing informational needs of the children in your community. Through youth networks, long-range planning data, and local media, you are continually gathering information on the demographics of your community, its economic and social conditions, and the informational and educational resources available. You are constantly evaluating the resources of your youth services department—the room itself, the collection, services, staff, management, and budget—in relation to this information.

Ideally, the resources available in your library correlate to the priority information needs of your community. Even with careful long-range planning, however, there is still likely to be a gap: funds may not exist to purchase urgently needed English-as-a-second-language materials for immigrant children, for example, or to provide vital library services to homeless children. How can you bridge this gap?

When library budgets do not stretch far enough to meet all of the priority information needs, there are really only three options: you can choose not to deliver the services, you can reduce other services, or you can seek alternative funding sources.

Asking for money is not a process many people cherish. Surely there is someone—a career administrator perhaps—who is better trained and has more time to do the dirty job of digging for dollars? But who better than you? The youth services manager has the best qualification of all: motivation. You are the one who recognizes the needs of your community, knows the services you want to provide, and knows how to provide them; therefore, you are ultimately the one who is responsible for making sure those needed services are provided. And you know the old saying, "if you want to get the job done right . . ."

Nonetheless, you need to know what you're getting into. What if you *do* get the money? Certainly, the services you need will be put into place. But grantsmanship is not just getting the money. Once procured there is additional work in supervising the services and activities that were the impetus for the grant, administering the grant, writing the reports, and so on. Take the time to be certain that the project is worth doing, and that you have the time to do it, *before* you get started.

At this point, you may be farther along than you realize. You know who you want to serve (Target Audience), and why (Needs Assessment). You know what you need to accomplish (Goals and Objectives), and you probably have a good idea of how you will accomplish it (Strategy for Implementation or Action Plan). You may even know how much it all will cost (Budget). You're familiar with the long-range planning process, so you know how to write goals and objectives, develop strategies, and measure success. These are the elements of the grants proposal. Fine-tuning them into a formal proposal to a specific organization will come after you have spent time researching and evaluating target sources. There are many possible sources of funding for library projects. Community service organizations, local businesses, private foundations, and state and federal grant programs can all provide financial support. Where you go for funding will be determined by the amount of money needed, the type of project you have developed, and the time frame under which you are working.

Where Are the Funds?

LSCA Grants

The most frequent source of funding for library services to youth is Library Services and Construction Act (LSCA) Title I grants. In fact, *Grant-Funded Projects for Library Youth Services 1985–1990* lists 322 projects, approximately 90 percent of which were funded through this source, while the other 10 percent received support from a variety of foundations, local safety and cultural councils, banks, and endowments.

LSCA funds are U.S. Department of Education monies that are administered through the state library agencies or other designated agencies. These funds are earmarked for "seed" and "demonstration" projects, and are available to libraries seeking to establish services that address the long-range, state-wide goals as developed by the state library agency. Currently LSCA funding is pending reauthorization by Congress. This may involve reprioritization or restructuring of the funding process. If you are considering applying for LSCA funds, be sure to clear this with your administration. Your library may be applying for more than one project; if so, your director will probably be asked to rank the applications in priority order. Discuss how your application will rank among those being prepared.

In addition, both the funding cycle and the amount of LSCA funds available to local libraries vary from state to state and from year to year. Ask your library director for this information, or contact your state library agency. The state consultants can help you determine whether your project is appropriate for LSCA funding and can tell you about similar projects. They may also be able to answer the following questions:

> Approximately how much money will be available for LSCA competitive grants this fiscal year? If there is only $100,000 available for the entire state, and your project requires $80,000, you may need to find another source or break your project into smaller chunks.

> Can you obtain a list of last year's grant projects? This list will give you information about the kinds of projects currently being funded in your state by LSCA funds and will also provide information about the average amount of grant awards, the distribution of awards throughout the state, and sources to contact for further information. This will give you some idea of the way your proposal will stack up against others statewide. Contact people who have received grants and request their opinions, insights, and copies of their successful proposals.

> What are the procedures and deadlines? An Intent to Apply may be required well in advance of your application. You will also need to know when applications will be available, when proposals will be due, and when announcements will be made. Knowing what the funding year will be for this grant cycle is also important. Usually, LSCA applications are available only once a year. The completed proposals are usually due within one to three months, and award announcements are made one to nine months later. Funding may begin immediately or as much as twelve months after the announcement. To succeed, your project must be able to work within these parameters.

If you determine that your project is not appropriate for LSCA funding, there are several alternatives to consider.

Foundation and Corporation Grants

The process of identifying serious corporate and foundation prospects involves both science and art. Several factors must be taken into consideration in determining whether it would be advisable for you to approach a particular corporation or foundation. In his book *Development Today: A Fund-Raising Guide for Non-Profit Organizations,* Jeffrey Lant describes the key factors:[1]

> If the prospect has guidelines (some don't), do they specifically exclude libraries or government agencies?

> Sources such as *The Foundation Directory, The National Directory of Corporate Giving,* and *The Big Book of Library Grant Money*

publish this information. However, these guidelines can and do change quickly. To be sure you're not wasting time, make a direct call to the foundation office and request up-to-date application guidelines.

Are you in the right geographic location for consideration? Most foundations and corporations fund projects within strict geographic areas.

Do you have a fund-raising objective (capital, program, operating) that the source can fund, or are your objectives unsuitable? *The Foundation Directory* lists the types of funds available from each foundation. Very little leeway is possible here. Make sure your project qualifies before going further.

Has the prospect given to you or to other libraries in the past? If so, did it indicate interest in giving to libraries again? Check with your administration about your library's past funding successes. Ask for a copy of the foundation's or corporation's annual report for information on past funding patterns.

Is there a specific reason why you think this funding source might be interested in the library? A foundation is something of a moving target—its priorities and interests are perpetually evolving. You must be aware of what their current interests are.

To come up with the best answers to these questions, it is helpful to know something about the varieties of corporate and foundation giving.

Independent foundations are grant-making organizations established to aid social, educational, religious, or other charitable activities. They are allowed broad discretionary giving, but may have specific guidelines and give only in a few specific fields. About 70 percent limit giving to their local area.

Company-sponsored foundations are grant-making organizations with close ties to the corporations providing funds. Their giving tends to be in fields related to the corporate activities or in communities where the corporation operates. They usually give more grants but in smaller dollar amounts than independent foundations.

Operating foundations use their resources to conduct research or provide a direct service. They make few, if any, grants. Grants generally are related directly to the foundation's program.

Community foundations are most often public-supported. They make grants for social, educational, religious, or other charitable purposes in a specific community or region. These grants are generally limited to charitable organizations in the local community.[2]

In approaching any type of foundation, research is essential. Find out as much as you can about the foundation, its patterns of giving, and its priorities. Furthermore, it is not enough simply to prepare and send a proposal—personal contact is crucial. Make direct contact with the professional staff. It is generally not difficult to get an appointment; it is their job to see you. But be sure to go prepared. Develop a one-page fact sheet about your project that you can hand to your contact that contains all of the relevant information in very concise form. This fact sheet can be left with the staff member for his or her future reference and will be used as the basis for your grant proposal (*see* figure 1).

Community-Based Funding

The local business community has a stake in the welfare of its citizenry. Business associations, chambers of commerce, banks, and individual businesses will often contribute services, goods, or funds to library projects. Civic and service organizations, such as Junior Leagues or Rotary, are also good sources of funds and volunteers.

The most important factor to consider in approaching any of these agencies is "what's in it for them." Always think in terms of how your project relates to your prospect's goals and objectives and how to make this a selling point in your proposal. Make your initial approach by finding out who to talk to, and then try to make an appointment for a personal visit to present your case. The fact sheet mentioned above will help you to make a professional, well-organized presentation. Some businesses will require that you submit a letter of request. This letter will act as a grant proposal in a letter format; therefore, it will include all of the elements of a formal grant application. You can simply write a cover letter, including the fact sheet, or you may wish to follow the example in figure 2 to help you prepare your letter.

In making requests from these organizations, try to keep reasonable goals in mind. Rather than trying to get $5,000 from one source, you may be more successful by asking ten sources for $500 each, or by making bequest amounts optional.

Community Coalitions

In recent years, the development of community collaboration, cooperation, and partnership has become increasingly important. By building a community funding coalition, you can call on expert help from a variety of sources. The purpose of the coalition is to identify and seek out sources of money and services needed for your project. It's an extension of networking—because "who you know" really does count. The DeKalb County Public Library, for example, has formed a coalition of local businesses; civic organizations; service organizations; and city, county, and state government agencies in support of Project Horizons (an outreach service to homeless shelters). Together, they provide the funding, services, and advice needed to make the project work. Businesses contribute volunteers, computers, books, computer repair and upkeep, bookshelves, filing cabinets, and money. Civic and service organizations provide volunteers, books, magazine subscriptions—and money. City and county schools have partnered with us to get state grant funds. And they all provide valuable referrals to further sources of help.

In order to form a coalition, you must look at your community to identify agencies and organizations who have a vested interest in your project. Use the same approach you would in contacting these agencies for full sponsorship: present a fact sheet, together with a list of the agencies

Fact Sheet:	**Building Blocks**
Sponsoring Agency:	DeKalb County Public Library
Program Coordinator:	Sherry Des Enfants, Youth Services Coordinator
	DeKalb County Public Library
	215 Sycamore Street
	Decatur, Georgia 30030
	(404)370-8450 FAX (404)370-8469

Purpose
To introduce parents and their very young children (ages 0–18 months) to the activities and materials which will enhance the development of infant language and motor skills.

Program
Building Blocks is an informal recreational and educational program for children ages 0–18 months and their parents. The program is currently offered at the Redan-Trotti Library, Reid H. Cofer Library, and the Decatur Library. It is scheduled to begin at the Flat Shoals Library and the Brookhaven in early 1994.

Each Building Blocks session includes a 45-minute "play-with-a-purpose" segment, during which parents and children are introduced to ways to interact meaningfully with infant and toddler toys such as blocks, gym tubes, tumble balls, and knobbed puzzles. The session is concluded with a 15-minute "linguistic" segment, during which the librarian models ways to share board books, movement games, songs, and nursery rhymes with very small children.

Resource lists of appropriate books, toys and audiovisual materials are distributed to parents to help them extend these experiences at home.

Need for Program
DeKalb County has accepted the challenge that President Bush presented to the nation with "America 2000:" Every parent in America will be a child's first teacher and devote time each day helping his or her preschool child learn; parents will have access to the training and support they need.

The first year of life is now generally recognized as the most important in the development of language skills. Parents can encourage their infants' language and cognitive development through simple and natural activities; however, the use of these activities is not an instinctive but a learned behavior. Studies indicate that many parents are not aware of the need for early learning activities and are not prepared to engage their children in them. These children enter public school up to two years behind their peers in preparedness for reading and are therefore already "at risk" for social and academic failure. Building Blocks is an important step in providing support and training to help parents become effective "first teachers."

Statistics
Families served: 15–20 families are expected to attend each session.

Request
A varied collection of at least 40 safe, durable, educational toys suitable for ages 0–18 months; board books and audiotapes are also needed for each library which offers the program. The toy collection will cost approximately $1,500.

Duration of Project
Building Blocks is an on-going project; a core collection of durable toys enables this project to carry on for 2–4 years before replacements are required.

Accomplishments of Building Blocks to Date
The first **Building Blocks** project was begun at the Redan-Trotti Library in March 1992 with a special Governor's Grant. The program is highly successful, with an average attendance of 56 people per session. Parents are very enthusiastic about the sessions, and have begun to bring and create their own toys to contribute to the program. Children began to exhibit social skills such as sharing, taking turns, and even waiting in line by the third session. Parents report that their children's vocabularies are growing quickly as the adults emulate the language behavior modelled by the librarian.

A spin-off of Building Blocks, called Building Blocks to Literacy, was funded by a Barbara Bush Foundation for Family Literacy grant in the Scottdale Child Development Center. This program incorporates the 60-minute session described above into a formal literacy program for low-literate teenage mothers. The goal is to teach the mothers to read so that they can read to their children, and to help them learn appropriate language-building activities. This project began in September of 1992; a video of Building Blocks to Literacy is available upon request.

Building Blocks on Wheels, an intergenerational outreach program for "high-risk" families, began in January 1993. This project delivers the program to homeless shelters, public health clinics, high school parenting classes, and community centers in DeKalb County. Building Blocks on Wheels is funded by a Federal LSCA Title I grant.

FIGURE 1. Fact Sheet

Dear Mr. Rotary President:

The DeKalb County Public Library is seeking $734 to fund Building Blocks to Literacy for one month. This is an award-winning intergenerational outreach program for at-risk families with one or more children ages 0–36 months.

The DeKalb County Public Library serves as the bridge that unites available, affordable, and accessible information with a widely diverse urban population of approximately 550,000 people. It works hand-in-hand with other agencies to provide access to the information and services integral to the well-being of our community. The Library has earned a national reputation for its innovative services and responsiveness to community needs. Awards include the 1991 National Association of Counties (NACo) Award for Project Horizons, which serves the literacy needs of children in homeless shelters; the 1991 American Library Association/Association for Library Service to Children Econo-Clad Award for Project Horizons; the 1993 H. W. Wilson Award for staff development; and the 1993 NACo Award for Building Blocks to Literacy.

Building Blocks to Literacy is funded through September 1993 by seed grants from the Barbara Bush Foundation for Family Literacy and LSCA Title I. It is designed to introduce at-risk families and their very young children to the activities and materials which will enhance the acquisition of language and cognitive skills in a playful, relaxed atmosphere. A part-time Senior Library Assistant takes the program to a minimum of seven easily accessible sites per week, including Nicholas House transitional homeless shelter, Clifton Springs Health Clinic, Crim High School and Decatur High School parenting classes, DeKalb EOA's Positive Generations program, South Decatur Community Center, Scottdale Child Development Center, and Fifth Avenue School's Evenstart program. At this time, the program reaches an average of 52 families each month.

Literacy begins in the cradle, when parents speak to, sing with, and share rhymes with their babies. These are simple, natural activities, but the use of them is a learned behavior, not an instinctive one. Studies indicate that many parents, notably those in "high-risk" situations, are not aware of the need for early learning activities, nor are they prepared to engage their children in them. These children enter school up to three years behind their peers in preparedness for reading, and are therefore already at risk for social and academic failure.

Building Blocks to Literacy empowers parents to be their child's first teacher. Each Building Blocks session includes a 45-minute "play-with-a-purpose" segment, during which parents and children are introduced to ways to build cognitive and linguistic concepts through play. This segment is followed by a 15-minute "linguistic" segment, during which successful methods of sharing language experiences such as board books, nursery rhymes, and song are modelled.

We are seeking to fund the cost of salary and FICA benefits for a 1/2FTE Senior Library Assistant for one month:

Salary: $8.52 per hr × 20 hrs per wk × 4 wks = $682
Benefits: FICA @ $.65 per hr × 20 hrs per wk × 4 wks = $52
TOTAL: $734

Other sources of support for this project are being sought through the area Rotary Clubs, the Decatur-DeKalb Chapter of 100 Black Women, the Georgia Power Foundation, and the BellSouth Foundation. The DeKalb County Public Library underwrites approximately $3,500 in administrative costs for this project, but it cannot support the personnel costs. The Library's operating budget sustained a 23% cut in FY92–93, and is expected to remain flat or be cut again in FY93–94. Without outside funding, the project will have to be discontinued.

Thank you for your consideration of this proposal. With your help, the cycle of failure can be broken, and a cycle of success built in its place.

Sincerely yours,

Sherry Des Enfants
Youth Services Coordinator

FIGURE 2.   A Proposal Letter for Funds to a Community Organization

who are already part of your coalition. Make sure that each prospective member understands that the organization will be part of a community effort. The interaction between these organizations is an important by-product of the coalition. Arrange to have meetings of the complete coalition at least every six months to enable this interaction, obtain feedback, provide evaluation, and facilitate brainstorming and problem solving.

Who Is Involved in the Grant Process?

Communication is vital to the success of any project. As you begin to develop your plans, make sure you are communicating with all of the relevant parties. Discuss your idea and the way you hope to implement it with your immediate supervisor and the administration. Be sure to relate your project to the library's long-range plan and demonstrate how it will support the library's mission and goals. Discuss possible funding sources with your administration and obtain permission to approach prospects. Remember, it is the library, not you, who will ultimately apply for the grant. In addition, talk with any library department heads who may be affected. Will materials be purchased through Acquisitions? Will these materials be processed through Cataloging? Will the proposed project increase Circulation or Reference requests? Then, once you have developed your idea, go back to these same people to present your complete concept. Be honest when making this presentation. Discuss the effect this project will have on staff, library resources, and patrons. Review the negative as well as the positive consequences so that administration can assess your project realistically.

Contact other agencies in your community that serve your target clientele. They can give you valuable help in developing appropriate and effective services and may also provide letters of support for your proposal. In addition, they can be instrumental in publicizing your project. Make connections with your prospective funding agency as well and work hard at sustaining them. Establish communication early and maintain it. Let people know as your plans change (and they *will* change). Provide every interested party with a copy of your finished proposal so that everyone knows exactly what will be expected of them if the project is funded and notify all of them immediately upon announcement of grant awards.

If your project is funded, communication will become even more vital. Your administration must know exactly what you are doing and how the project is being handled. It cannot be emphasized enough that the *library* receives the award, not you personally.

What Makes a Grant Project Successful?

Winning projects depend on careful planning, a complete understanding of the problem, and consideration of alternate solutions. Without these elements, you're bound to misfire. When asking for money, you have to be thoroughly prepared. Potential funding agencies range from your local garden club to the Coca Cola Foundation to the federal government, but they all share a common characteristic: they want to know that you know what you're doing. You can only prove that by doing your research and thinking through each step thoroughly. The research you do at this stage may later be incorporated into a formal grant proposal, a fact sheet, a proposal letter, or may be simply used in talking informally with the president of your Friends group, but it is essential to success.

Here are some of the questions that funders will ask when evaluating your proposal:

Is there a need for it?

Is anyone else doing what you propose or employing your general approach?

Is the idea sound?

Is the project feasible?

Will there be significant benefits—locally, regionally, nationally?

Do you and your library staff have the knowledge, skill, and experience to carry out your plan?

Will the library be able to continue the project or activity after the funding period?

Are the resources and time sufficient for carrying out the activity?

Is the proposed strategy cost-effective and how can this be demonstrated?

Can you demonstrate community cooperation and involvement?

To answer these questions, start by looking around. "Looking around" may sound familiar. It is the basic first step in the long-range planning process. Dig out your copy of *Planning and Role Setting for Public Libraries,* and let it guide you through the data collection process. *Output Measures for Public Library Service to Children* also provides many strategies for collecting and interpreting relevant data.

You will need to do some research. Find out as much as you can about your target clientele. Gather data from the census, your local school system, and area service groups to answer the following questions: What specific ages are you targeting, and how many children of that age are in your service area? What ethnic populations will you be reaching? Which disabilities will be represented in the target group? What is the median income and educational level of the families in your target group? What other agencies serve this clientele, and in what ways?

Determine the needs of your target clientele and how the library can meet those needs. You may have already intuitively recognized a specific need, but documentation and hard data are needed to substantiate your assessment. Use census data, focus groups, library output measures, and surveys as sources of information.

Figure out how much it will cost to meet those needs. This is tricky. Let's say you're trying to acquire Spanish-language materials for preschoolers. You may think all you need to know is the cost of the books and tapes. However, you also need to find out how much cataloging and processing will cost, as well as address the personnel issue: who will select the materials and deliver the services? Will you need new signage? Will you publish bibliographies? Do you have adequate shelving for this collection, or will it need to be purchased? All of these steps are cost factors and must be figured into your budget.

Obviously, determining the cost requires careful consideration of the entire project. In this case, you would need to consult with technical services, acquisitions, print shop, and probably payroll to reach a total. You would also need to survey the children's room to be sure of shelving space and signage needs. Find out if the library can absorb the cost of some items listed in this scenario, such as your time in selection of materials, or acquisitions staff time. These budget items will be listed as the library's contribution to the project, so they cannot be taken for granted.

Gather information about your library and the staff who will be implementing the project. Job descriptions and resumes are often required as part of the proposal package in order to demonstrate the quality of staff. Your library's track record with other alternative funding sources can help you prove that the organization is reliable and capable.

You've collected your data, and you've decided on a plan of action. You know how much it's going to cost, and you know who you're going to approach for the funding. Now you're ready to write your grant proposal.

How Do You Write a Grant Proposal?

Several potential funding agencies have been discussed in this chapter, and each has its own requirements for application. But the most common approach to these agencies is the written proposal: a document that tells the potential funding agency exactly who you are, whom you are serving, what their needs are, how you plan to meet these needs, how much these services will cost, and how you will evaluate the success of your project.

Writing a grant proposal is not as hard as you may have heard. In fact, you've already done the hardest parts. Now, you just put what you know into a specified written format. Start by finding out exactly what those specifications are. Each application package is basically the same, but each has its own peculiarities. Read through the application instructions carefully, then read them again. List the requirements and follow them exactly. For instance, the application may specify one-inch margins, double-spaced, no more than sixty characters per line. Do not vary; you'll only be cheating yourself. The evaluators may not even consider your application if you do not follow the rules.

Title Page

Most applications include a title page form. It sounds redundant, but read the instructions for filling out this form and follow them. It makes a very bad first impression if you put your own name where the library director's name was supposed to be.

This page usually has a place for the director's signature, and sometimes that of the chair of the governing board of trustees. Be sure to submit your complete proposal to your director in plenty of time for it to be read and for corrections and modifications to be made before it is signed. Do not expect the director to sign or submit to the board an incomplete or inaccurate proposal. Be aware of the fact that your director or the chair may not be available at the last minute—plan ahead!

Abstract

The abstract or summary is the first thing to be read but the last thing to be written. Since it will provide the reader's first and last impressions of the proposed project, it is one of the most important single elements of the proposal.

Abstracts are usually limited to one page or less, but they must state what the project will do, who the clientele will be, and how the project will be accomplished (including measurable objectives). The abstract is often handled separately in processing, so it must be capable of speaking for the proposal when it is separated from it.

A clear, concise abstract should include the following:

Identification of the applicant and a phrase or two about the applicant's credibility (at least one sentence)

The reason for the grant request: issue, problem, or need to be met (at least one sentence)

The objectives to be achieved through this funding

The kinds of activities to be conducted to accomplish these objectives

The total cost of the project, funds already committed, and amount asked for in this proposal (if requested)

Statement of Need or Needs Assessment

This is your chance to convey a sense of urgency for doing what you want to do. State the problem in terms of the needs of the patrons, not the library. Start with a direct, powerful statement, then elaborate using facts and figures. You cannot rely on instinct or vague statements—corroborate every fact and give a source for every quote.

In this section, you will identify your target clientele, citing number and characteristics of the population to be served and how the target group was chosen; describe the need for library service and how it was determined, and explain why this need should be a funding priority. Use clearly labeled charts, diagrams, and graphics to document your claims.

Do not assume that your reader will know anything about libraries, library services, literacy, or literature. Use no technical jargon without definition.

Goals and Objectives

For anyone who has been involved in the long-range planning process, this section will be easy. The process of developing goals and objectives is exactly the same for grant proposals as for branch libraries. Although a few applications do not require goals and objectives, develop them and state them anyway. They will provide the framework for the entire proposal, and will help you to focus your project.

Your goals will state the overall aims of the project. They should flow from the Needs Statement and should be stated in terms of the benefit to the target group, not to the library; however, you should show how the goals of your project relate to the long-range plans of your library. For example,

> Parents and their very young children will be introduced to the activities and materials that will enhance the acquisition of language and cognitive skills.

> *is better than*

> The library will provide activities and materials to enhance the acquisition of language and cognitive skills.

Remember that goals are long-range, timeless, broad in scope. Goals are moving targets, not measurable or necessarily attainable. They are the umbrella statement of intent. Try to limit yourself to one or two goals—too many goals indicate a poorly focused project.

Your objectives must be measurable. Objectives describe specific outcomes or expectations. They must be clearly written and understandable, not open to a variety of interpretations. Your objectives must indicate a specific time frame, and be achievable. For example,

> To deliver Building Blocks instruction on location to at least sixteen sites per month during FY 1992–93.

Planning and Role Setting for Public Libraries provides a recipe book for developing functional goals and objectives.

Strategy for Implementation, or Action Plan

This part of the narrative explains to your potential funding agency exactly how you expect to achieve the goals and objectives you have set forth. It's easy to get bogged down in this section, because it's all detail. You need to be as logical and jargon-free as possible, and demonstrate to your reader how the procedures and activities you are describing will meet the needs of your target audience.

Start by describing the content of your program in laymen's terms. Explain exactly what will happen and why, justifying any hiring of personnel, purchasing of equipment, or contractual services your plan will require. Estimate the number of titles or volumes to be purchased, and in what subject areas. Then state in sequence the activities and procedures to be used in meeting each objective.

My favorite approach to this section is to detail a single objective at a time. This way, the reader has no trouble in correlating an activity to a specific objective. The last thing you want is to irritate the reader by forcing him to flip back and forth between the sections trying to make it all make sense. Do everything you can to make the proposal read smoothly and logically.

In this approach, each objective is briefly restated, followed by a detailed, chronological list of the activities needed to implement this objective. The persons responsible for implementation of each activity are listed, and a resume or job description for each person is appended. For example:

Obj. 3. To provide one deposit paperback book collection (approximately three books per average juvenile capita) in each shelter by October 1, 1993.

a. Project Coordinator (please see resume and job description, appendix I) identifies and purchases approximately 900 juvenile paperback titles for deposit collections by August 15, 1993.

b. Library Assistant (please see job description, appendix II) processes books upon arrival, stamping Project Horizons identification in each book.

c. Library Assistant contacts shelters by September 15, 1993, arranging for deposits and determining the current average juvenile population and age range.

d. Library Assistant selects appropriate materials for each shelter and delivers collections by October 1, 1993.

e. Library Assistant monitors collection on a weekly basis, rotating and replacing materials as necessary.

f. Library Assistant maintains weekly statistics on use of collection.

A time line or tasking chart is often required. This can be as simple as the example in figure 3.

Be sure to build preparation time into your plan. For instance, if you will be hiring, allow time to advertise the position, schedule and conduct interviews, and make a decision.

Task	Person Responsible	Date Due
purchase books	coordinator	8/15/93
process books	library assistant	9/15/93
contact shelters	library assistant	9/15/93
select appropriate books for shelters	library assistant	9/30/93
deliver books to shelters	library assistant	10/1/93
monitor collections	library assistant	weekly 10/93–8/94

FIGURE 3.   Tasking Chart

Do everything you can to make your strategy understandable to your reader. It must be very clear what you are going to do, how you are going to do it, and why you need to spend the money. Make sure that every line item in your budget request is referred to somewhere in this section.

Evaluation

Your evaluation plan explains how you will determine whether or not your project is actually accomplishing the goals and objectives you have set forth.

Your plan should provide for the assessment to be ongoing throughout the life of the project, monitoring how well implementation is progressing, and providing opportunity for change if needed. The evaluation should allow you to determine the impact of your services on the target group, and, ultimately, whether or not the project was worth doing.

In this section, describe what methodology will be employed to measure the effectiveness of each objective, who will conduct the appraisal, and why that person was selected to do the evaluation. It is advisable to restate each objective, then describe the evaluation techniques that will be applied to it so that the reader can clearly see how your plan is tied to the goals and objectives. For example:

> Obj. 2. To motivate 95 percent of parents to involve children in independent literacy activities.
>
> Parents will be required to maintain and present a record of their independent sessions with their children (see "Reading with Children," appendix IV). A minimum of five hours of reading activities is required. Staff contact by Senior Library Assistant for six months following program will monitor further involvement.

Be as complete as possible: if surveys will be conducted, include a copy of the survey questions in your application packet; if data will be collected, include a copy of the data collection form. These materials will indicate to the reader that you have thought through your plan completely and are prepared to implement it.

Output Measures for Public Library Service to Children provides valuable measurement tools that may be used or adapted to evaluate your project. Try to include qualitative as well as quantitative measures—it doesn't really matter how many children you serve as long as you do it well.

Budget

Grant applications contain two budget sections—the narrative and budget form. The narrative section describes and justifies the budget request. This section is not necessarily in paragraph form, but instead should be formatted to provide the required information in the clearest possible way. The narrative should include personnel and proposed salaries and benefits and the number of hours committed to the project; type and cost of supplies and equipment; estimated mileage; type and cost of library materials; cataloging and processing cost of library materials, etc. Be sure to distinguish between grant-funded costs and library-funded costs by creating separate narrative sections for each. Your narrative section should also provide the formulas you used to determine costs. This will enable your reader to calculate the adequacy and accuracy of your request. For example:

Federal LSCA Title VI Funds

a. Salary and Wages
   This position is fully dedicated to the literacy project (100% of the total 1,040 hours of the contract).

   1/2FTE Senior Library Assistant
   Hourly salary @ $8.52 × 20 hrs per wk × 52 wks = $8,861

b. Fringe Benefits (FICA only)
   1/2FTE Senior Library Assistant
   Hourly salary @ $8.52 × .0765 × 20 hrs per wk
   × 52 wks = $678

In preparing your budget, be sure to read and comply with the budget restrictions. Application packages will include definitions for each category, particularly personnel, travel, equipment, and supplies. Your budget must conform to these restrictions in order to be considered.

The budget form is usually straightforward. It will be divided into line items, and will also be divided into "grant funds" and "local," or "matching," funds. Local funds indicate the commitment your library will make toward the support of this project. Local funds should be discussed thoroughly with your administration before commitment.

It is important to review your proposed budget with your director and your library's fiscal manager before typing it on the form. Discuss your narrative and your budget form, ascertaining accuracy and completeness.

Appendices

Your appendices will include

1. Charts, diagrams, and maps referred to in the Needs Assessment. These should be clearly labeled and their origins cited.
2. Job descriptions and resumes. Any proposed positions to be funded should be accompanied by a complete job description, including required qualifications.
3. Letters of support from cooperating agencies. Contact cooperating agencies well in advance to secure letters of support. Tell them precisely what to include in their letter—you may even provide a sample for them. The letters should be addressed to you, explaining why they are in support of your plans and how they will cooperate.

4. Any required materials: i.e., certification of IRS tax status, list of board members, etc.

The application instructions may specify a particular organization for this section; if not, organize it as logically as possible. Try to place items in the order they are referenced in the document, and identify each one clearly.

What Happens Next?

You've completed the proposal, made the correct number of copies, and sent them off to the funding agency by certified mail. You've made copies for yourself, your administration, and all cooperating agencies. What happens next? There are actually three possible results of your application: (1) your proposal is denied, (2) your proposal is accepted pending budget or program revision, or (3) your proposal is funded.

If your proposal is denied, don't consider this a failure. Do consider it a learning experience. Talk to the funding agency. Find out why the request was denied, and what will improve it. Then make those improvements, and resubmit—to that agency, or another one.

In "Guidelines for Grantseekers," Leighton Cluff, president of the Robert Wood Johnson Foundation, gives some insight into why a grant application is turned down:[3]

It is outside the purview of the funding agency. Either you failed to familiarize yourself with the funding restrictions and areas of interest, or misunderstood them.

The subject is not relative to the priorities of the agency. Your project may be too narrow in focus, or too broad, to relate to the priorities. It may miss them altogether.

The methodology appears flawed. You may be approaching the problem in a way that does not appear to adequately address the needs. This could be because of inadequate staffing, poor recruitment techniques, etc.

The agency is not the most appropriate funding source. A question asked constantly in the review of proposals is, "Why should we be the source for this funding?" If another agency would be more appropriate, you can sometimes be referred to that source.

Similar programs are already being funded. You can be too late with a good proposal.

All of these problems can be solved by doing your homework: talking with your funding agency ahead of time, researching your problem and its possible solutions, reading the literature. If you didn't do that the first time around, do it now and try again. Don't give up. A lot of proposals don't get approved; however, many get refined, reworked, resubmitted—and funded.

Sometimes a funding agency will approve the basic proposal, but will request revision of the budget or the program. When this occurs, communicate clearly with the funding agency and with your administration to arrive at a plan that suits all concerned. Remember that program modifications will usually affect the budget, so make sure that your revised version includes a new budget if necessary.

If your proposal is approved, congratulations! Your work has just begun. Here's how to hit the ground running: Funding often begins very quickly on the heels of the announcement, so you need to be ready to begin almost on a moment's notice. Even before you know whether or not the project is funded, there are steps you can take to prepare. Don't worry, the work won't go to waste—you'll use it when you do get funding down the line. If you have planned well, there will be ample preparation time built into your schedule for the kinds of things that can only be done at the last minute, such as advertising a position. Other things can be done in advance, however, to ensure that your project flows smoothly.

If you are hiring, become thoroughly familiar with the hiring process of your library. Talk with your personnel officer to ensure that you are prepared, and that you comply with all regulations. You will already have a job description for any positions for which you will hire. You may also need a contract—check with your administration to find out if one is needed. If so, sample ones may already be on file that can help you draft your own, or research may be required.

Make a complete list of all items to be purchased. Will you have to go through a bid process? If so, do your groundwork. If not, go ahead and make your selections and write up your orders. You'll be ready to submit as soon as funding is available.

Maintain contact with all of your cooperating agencies. Tell them where you are in the review process. As soon as funding is announced, schedule a meeting with them to begin putting your plan into action.

Running a grant project while maintaining regular library services can feel very much like one of those famous juggling acts where the little clown tries to keep all of the plates intact. You have a feeling something is going to crash. It doesn't need to happen. If you've done your groundwork, and hit the ground running, your plans should be well on their way to fruition. Remember the time line you developed? Consult it regularly, and stick with the schedule. Have regular meetings with all of the people involved in order to maintain an awareness of all elements of the project. You'll be evaluating and reevaluating your plan as you go along, so you'll have plenty of time to recognize any problems and react accordingly.

Don't panic if your plans have to change—they nearly always do. What looks good on paper will usually require a few adjustments in reality, and your funding agency is aware of that. It's so common, in fact, that most agencies include instructions for what to do under these circumstances in their notification packages. The important thing is communication. Notify your funding agency in writing of the need for change and the precise ways in which you plan to modify your original concept. If these modifications alter an objective, for example, state your new objective, the strategy for implementation, and how you will evaluate success. If your plans require you to alter the budget by moving funds from one category to another, you should submit a revised budget to your funding agency. The budget should indicate what the original allocations were, contrasted with the proposed changes. Justifications for variations must be included.

You should receive either written or verbal approval for your change-of-plan before you proceed. File the written approval with a copy of the written request; you will need these for your final report. If only verbal approval is received, note who gave you permission, along with the date and time, on the copy of your request. All changes, proposed and approved, should also be communicated with your administration and with the cooperating agencies. Give them a chance to discuss your plans before you make the change, and let them know the results afterward. Keep everyone on the same page.

Reporting

Each agency has its own requirements and schedule for reporting, but there are some generalities to keep in mind. Most agencies require both a narrative and a financial report. The narrative section should detail:

Program progress toward meeting the objectives. State each objective, what you have done to accomplish it, and the results. Provide positive statistics based on the measurement criteria described in your proposal.

Explanation of changes in program direction. There should be no surprises here; the agency should be fully aware of the modifications you have made and why. Refer to the original communication as much as possible, using the same language and justifications. Keep copies of all communications on file in case of future audit.

Description of project strengths and weaknesses. Here's your chance to brag—but only if what you brag about can be documented. Use at least one "human-interest" anecdote if possible. Include photos, letters from participants, brochures, newspaper clippings, etc. Make your program come alive for your reader. This is also the time to be honest. Explain what didn't work and why. Suggest ways to improve the project next time around.

Evaluation documentation. Provide statistical forms, survey instruments and results, etc., to document your evaluation, along with an interpretation of data.

The financial report must demonstrate that you spent the money exactly the way you said you'd spend the money. The agency will usually provide a form for the financial report, to be submitted along with documentation, such as receipts, vouchers, and invoices. The financial report should indicate the amount of each original line item allocation, the actual expenditure in each line item, and justify any variations. Include copies of all correspondence concerning budget modifications.

In Conclusion

Writing a grant proposal is very similar to what you do every day: identifying needs, and finding ways to meet those needs. Librarians are in a good position to write grants. Writing a grant may take your job or your perception of it to a higher level. So, pull out that wish list of services you'd like to offer your patrons "if only . . . ," and make those wishes come true!

Notes
1. Jeffrey Lant, *Development Today: A Fund-Raising Guide for Non-Profit Organizations,* 4th ed. (Cambridge, Mass.: JLA Publications, 1990), 93.

2. National Society of Fund Raising Executives, "Looking at the Beast," *National Society of Fund Raising Executives Quarterly Newsletter* (Winter 1990):20.

3. Leighton Cluff, "Guidelines for Grantseekers" (Robert Wood Johnson Foundation, n.d.).

Bibliography

Big Book of Library Grant Money. Prepared by The Taft Group for the American Library Association. Chicago: American Library Association, 1994.

Catalog of Federal Domestic Assistance, 27th ed. Washington, D.C.: Supertintendent of Documents, U.S. Government Printing Office, 1993.

Foundations Directory. New York: Foundation Center, 1993.

Foundation Fundamentals, 4th ed. New York: Foundation Center, 1991.

Foundation Grants Index, 21st ed. New York: Foundation Center, 1993.

Geller, Bob. *Plain Talk about Grants,* rev. ed. Sacramento, Calif.: California State Library Foundation, 1988.

Grant-Funded Projects for Library Youth Services 1985–1990. Chicago: ALSC/ American Library Association, 1993.

Hall, Mary. *Getting Funded: A Complete Guide to Proposal Writing,* 3d ed. Portland, Oreg.: Continuing Education Publications, Portland State Univ., 1988.

How to Use the Catalog of Federal Domestic Assistance, expanded version. Los Angeles, Calif.: The Grantsmanship Center, 1989.

Margolin, Judith M. *Foundation Center's User-Friendly Guide,* 2d ed. New York: Foundation Center, 1992.

McClure, Charles R., Amy Owen, Douglas L. Zweizig, Mary Jo Lynch, and Nancy A. Van House. *Planning and Role Setting for Public Libraries: A Manual of Options and Procedures.* Chicago: American Library Association, 1987.

National Directory of Corporate Giving, 2d ed. New York: Foundation Center, 1991.

Walter, Virginia A. *Output Measures for Public Library Service to Children: A Manual of Standardized Procedures.* Chicago: American Library Association, 1992.

Chapter 4

Youth Services Policies and Procedures

Mary M. Wagner and Gretchen Wronka

One of the tasks I was assigned when hired a year ago as children's coordinator was to review, revise, and fill in the gaps in our policies and procedures. But I haven't had time!

We're really dealing with some discipline problems in one of our branches. We have rules of conduct posted which are clear, but somehow we need to make these rules a part of our policies. It is hard for the staff to enforce rules and be the "friendly" librarian without having a statement about why we require certain behaviors.

Regardless of how well I prepare to present a new policy for the Board's approval, I never know how they will react and what policy I will end up living with as well as administering.

Give youth services librarians the chance to talk about library policy and they will! From around the country, they express similar concerns. While acknowledging that good policy is essential to defining service, they admit that there are significant barriers, attitudinal as well as institutional, that prevent youth services librarians from making policy development a priority.

This chapter will discuss the role of policy and procedure development in defining youth services in public libraries. As background for the chapter, Wagner and Wronka surveyed youth services librarians and co-ordinators, state agency consultants, and library directors with previous youth services experience (*see* Appendix at the end of this chapter). The respondents had all participated in recent sessions of the Managing Children's Services Discussion Group of the Association for Library Service to Children (ALSC), a division of the American Library Association (ALA).

The purpose of the survey was to discover how these individuals had been involved in the development of policies specific to youth services; what incidents or experiences had led to the need for such policies; the process used to develop the policies; and the steps taken to facilitate policy approval and implementation. The survey also examined the relationship between a library's policies and its philosophy of service, both in terms of children and young people in general and in reaction to perceived "problem" behavior.

In addition to the telephone survey, a literature search was conducted. Personal experiences were also incorporated.

Policies

Because policies may sometimes seem more punitive than productive, it is necessary to define a middle ground in policy development. Policies should help library users feel comfortable, not guilty or incompetent. They can broadly express a library's philosophy of service and protect both staff and patrons through equitable guidelines and accompanying procedures. They can also set the tone for how staff interacts with library users.

In this discussion of the policy development process, examples of specific policies are used sparingly. While useful, sample policies are not always adaptable to the needs of a particular library. Because sample policies may serve the function of defining the issues needing examination, the bibliography includes titles that provide numerous examples for this purpose.

There is evidence of growing professional interest in policy discussion throughout the American Library Association. Most recently, the Public Library Association (PLA) has established its Public Policy for Public Libraries Section. Queries for policy examples have been posted on various Internet discussion lists. The need for policy in the areas of appropriate library behavior, unattended and latchkey children, and access to materials is addressed throughout the current library literature. Multicultural and gender-fair philosophies and data privacy issues as they relate to minors raise new subject areas for potential policy formulation.

The librarians contacted unanimously expressed the need for clear policy statements. At the same time, they commented frequently on the lack of time to adequately review existing policies or develop new ones. Librarians who spend most of their time working directly with children and their advocates focused primarily on practical policies such as those that define patron behavior or set rules for library card registration. Librarians approaching the issue from a more managerial perspective tended to describe the need for policies that define a philosophy of service and provide guidelines for the development of procedures.

Those surveyed also described a whole range of new policies reflecting such current social realities as child molestation, neglect, or homelessness. Several librarians noted that an increased concern for the safety of children has even generated discussion about access to the children's room. The library policy described by one youth services librarian does not allow adults to read, study, or even just sit in the children's room unless accompanied by a child. Special permission is required for adults such as teachers to use the children's room. Unaccompanied adults are required to take children's books to other areas in the library.

While most states do not require library staff to report suspected abuse, one respondent described staff concern that there has been an observable increase in abuse of children by parents or caregivers in the library. This may begin with the adults insulting or yelling at the children, but it often escalates into hitting or slapping. Library staff in that system met with social workers to gain input on developing a child abuse policy. The social workers emphasized the necessity of having such a policy. For many families there exists a need to know the parameters of acceptable library behavior. Clear and positively stated library rules leave less potential for frustrated and insecure adults to overreact to their child's often perfectly appropriate library behavior. They also stressed that policies and procedures need to clarify under what circumstances it is appropriate for staff to intervene in such situations. As a result of this policy, ongoing workshops have been conducted to increase staff confidence by giving them practical techniques to use when enforcing the policy.

While the need for policies is generally recognized, there are some barriers to policy development. One extreme that the survey respondents described was youth services librarians who find policy development and implementation boring and bureaucratic. When they feel that excessive demands are already being placed on them, they wonder why they should give attention to policy development, which they see as the role of managers. They would rather provide direct service to children and young people than to develop clear, concise, and useful policy statements, even though such statements might actually do much to improve the quality of those services.

At the other end of the spectrum are the librarians who find security in policy and who spend an inordinate amount of time solving potential problems by developing tedious, redundant, and punitive policies. Current rules as arcane as "You may not get a library card until you can print both your first and last names," conjure up images of Eleanor Estes's character, Rufus Moffit, and his library frustrations.[1] As discussed earlier, there must be middle ground in policy development.

The impetus for policy statements usually comes about in one of two ways: either in response to a particular situation or a series of events that have caused problems; or out of thoughtful planning in conjunction with the development of mission or goal statements for youth services. In the first model, policy is seen as a reaction to a problem and as a solution to it. In the second model, policy is a reflection of the philosophy of service to children held by the entire library staff and helps shape the services provided. The foresight implied in the second model makes the policies developed ultimately more useful. "If you have a policy in place and something happens, you can be proactive rather than reactive," noted a state consultant.

Some of the librarians with whom we spoke have no specific policies for children but rather perceive children as library users in the same way in which adults are perceived as library users. A coordinator of youth services in a large urban area warns, however, that in these cases it "is important that youth services librarians sit on all committees that make policy since all policy ultimately affects children." Several respondents emphasized that when youth services staff are involved in policy development, they are more willing to take an active role in implementing the resulting policy.

One librarian remarked that it was also essential to involve the complete spectrum of staff in the development of these common policies, particularly emphasizing support staff. "If the circulation staff is having a problem with rules that the librarians have set, what might have been easy turns into a nightmare," she said.

For the same reasons, the development of policies that are specific to youth services must also include the involvement of the entire staff. Indeed, support staff may be the first to identify situations that need policy revision or development. For instance, circulation staff in a large suburban system were concerned that some children of divorced parents were being restricted in their use of library materials. Children living with custodial parents and having library cards were not allowed by those parents to use the card while visiting noncustodial parents. To alleviate embarrassment and to make visits to any library as comfortable as possible, the system modified the registration policy to allow children to hold two library cards, one for each of their households. The policy also applies to children in foster homes, allowing them a card for the home address and another for the foster family address. The written policy is implemented on a situational basis and the support staff makes the determination about issuing cards as they see the need.

During the process of developing youth services policies, it is necessary to examine thoroughly their impact on all library services, not only how they affect youth services. Policy development also provides the opportunity for administration and staff to reflect on how all services are integrated.

As an example, one coordinator described responding to concerns expressed by branch managers as well as by youth services librarians by developing a system-wide policy that states it is the responsibility of all staff to help children with their homework. This clarified reference expectations in a definitive policy that was then incorporated into the system reference policy.

One library system convened a youth services advisory committee including representatives of the branches as well as the central library. This advisory committee allows for the development of youth services policy that is consistent with the library's philosophy of service as well as tying policy to the stated mission, purpose, and goals of the library and thereby makes the policies internally consistent. It also allows for the resolution of differences on sensitive issues. This group meets annually to review existing policies, evaluate the results of policy implementation, and recommend changes or additions to the policy. An entire day is scheduled for this exercise to allow enough time for achieving consensus on proposed changes. The recommendations from this advisory committee are then forwarded to the administration for approval and implementation. A check-list of steps involved in policy development is given in figure 1.

At times, the process of policy development can become enormously political. Policies initiated by youth services librarians and managers need to be supported and approved by managers and librarians of other depart-ments as well as by support staff, volunteers, and others involved in the implementation of the policies. Collegial awareness and approval can also help facilitate administrative approval.

Youth services librarians have the responsibility for building that sup-port. It is essential that they recognize that youth services are not isolated from the rest of the library and that problems encountered in the children's room are often encountered in other areas.

Often the final approval of all library policies, including youth services policies, resides with the board of trustees. Youth services librarians often walk a thin line during this approval process. Library administrators may be reluctant to allow staff to present their views to board members directly. However, if an open procedure that incorporates discussion and consensus-building is followed during the process of policy development, a trust level between staff and administration can be achieved. This is essential when presenting a united front to the board.

It is important to recognize that some policy statements have the potential to become political footballs in the community, subject to po-litical whims. Sensitive issues that may polarize the community are often more difficult to address at the board level than at the administrative level, especially when it comes to youth services.

One coordinator spoke of efforts to revise the policy requiring on-site parental signatures for library cards. The board "will not budge" from its

---

The following checklist may be useful in reviewing steps for developing policy statements:

Develop library and youth services mission statements and roles statements in context of all library services

Review existing library policies in light of the mission and roles statements

Involve staff and board in identifying new policy needs

Conduct literature search and examine sample policies

Draft policy. Review and revise after staff discussion

Finalize policy. Seek administrative approval, followed by board approval

Determine implementation timeline, resources needed, and individuals responsible for implementation

Identify and develop necessary procedures to implement policy

Inform library users of both policy and procedures

Develop process for periodic review and evaluation of policy and procedures

---

FIGURE 1.   Policy Development Checklist

position that this is an issue of finances, not access. Board members are concerned that if a parent does not sign the card, no one is responsible for lost or damaged materials. At the same time, minors in that system may check out R-rated videos because the parental signature requirement reinforces another policy that holds parents responsible for being aware of what their children are checking out.

It is necessary to ensure that board members understand the principles underlying politically sensitive policies, particularly regarding First Amendment issues. Library administration and staff are responsible for educating board members about the implications of their decisions on library service. For instance, well-meaning board members might agree with public opinion which holds that libraries should not allow children access to certain books or audiovisual materials, despite the negative precedent that this would set in terms of broader questions of access. An informed board will be more successful in dealing with community issues as they apply to library policy.

The trustees of one library system sponsored a public forum on children's access to library materials. The intention was to examine how the library could work together with parents to help children use the library in ways that conform to their own family values. The priority of the Board Policy Committee, which considered many policy changes recommended at the forum, was "to help families use the library according to their own value systems without infringing on the rights of other families who may have different value systems."[2] After analyzing all of the suggested policy changes, the Board Policy Committee made its recommendations to the full board for adoption.

Another proactive way of using the board approval process was described by one of the respondents who is currently shepherding through a new policy on services to children in groups. In this particular system, the process is tied to the revision of the five-year plan, for which staff, board, and the public were surveyed about general topical issues currently affecting library services. Each issue is being discussed by a committee composed of staff and one board member. Ultimately, the goals and objectives resulting from the committees will be prioritized, and policies necessary to implement them will be developed. This coordinator pointed to the problem identified by the increased demand from schools and child care centers to schedule library visits: current policy requiring parents to sign their children's library cards in the library. Under the umbrella of increasing access to the library for all children, the subcommittee considering the youth services issues decided that revising this policy is an absolutely essential objective. The subcommittee was shown examples of other systems' policies on services to children in groups and heard from several other coordinators and public desk youth services librarians who spoke from experience on the effectiveness as well as the drawbacks of these policies. Using these practical examples, the coordinator was able to answer the "what if" kinds of questions from subcommittee members.

This coordinator speaks with enthusiasm about the participation of board members on these planning and policy development committees. She noted, "Since the board has to defend the long-range plan to the commissioners, being on the committees developing the plan and necessary policies helps enormously in the board's education process."

Board members' understanding of library policy does, indeed, make them more effective in representing the library to the public and bringing the public's concerns to library administration. Explained one librarian, "Policies create the environment to accomplish the library's goals. In our library that means giving everyone the best possible experience." Library board members who not only understand policy but are involved in its development are true partners with library staff and administration as services are developed that best meet the community's library and information needs.

Procedures

Policy is the *why* of doing something—the clarification of a library's philosophy and mission. Procedures, on the other hand, are the practical guides that instruct the staff how to handle specific situations. Both are necessary for effective and efficient services for children and young people. Procedures can minutely prescribe staff behavior and do not require board actions, so they are much more easily revised or modified than policy. They must be consistently applied, but must also be flexible enough to adapt to the everyday reality of library life.

One librarian described the unique process her library uses for discussing sensitive issues that may require changes in policy or procedures. Rather than beginning with elaborate policy statements, when staff initially identify their concerns, a committee is charged to develop procedures. Based on the effectiveness of these procedures, the committee then decides on the need for policy.

The changing social climate has meant drastic changes in procedures as well as policy. For instance, in years past it was not uncommon for library staff to drive a child home if no parent had appeared at closing time. Such kindness is almost unthinkable today and not because library staff are any less concerned about the child's welfare. Personal and institutional liability issues make such actions impossible.

Many libraries now have specific procedures requiring staff to call the police when children are left unattended. These kinds of procedures are often hard for staff to accept, since they go against the nurturing grain common to the profession. However, establishing such procedures is ultimately in the best interest of the child as well as library staff.

One issue that straddles both policy and procedural areas is how to publicize the new guidelines. Several librarians who have developed specific procedures for abandoned children raised the issue of how best to inform the public of the existence of such procedures. They described attempts to post policy statements in public areas and emphasized that they inform parents and caregivers of the procedure as the situation warrants. One library's procedures include giving a copy of the policy to the police officer who picks up the child and requesting that the officer give the policy to the child's parents when returning the child to their care.

Most of the youth services librarians surveyed indicated that their preferred method of educating the public was to discuss the policy when the need to invoke it arises. This often involves the need to "practice assertive public service," one librarian said emphatically. For instance, in restricting adult use of the children's room, staff approach unaccompanied adults, asking if they need help and strongly suggesting that they take their juvenile reading materials to an adult reading area. When placed in the context of children's safety, the coordinator reported that few adults argue or question the policy.

Procedures should be developed with common sense and should not be used to restrict an individual staff member's professional judgment. Regarding potential child abuse in the library, one librarian commented, "There are no easy answers, and no matter how much training is provided or how many policies are approved, the bottom line is that staff ultimately have to decide how to respond to each situation. We have procedures, but they are only guidelines to be interpreted by library staff with common sense and the responsibility that applies to staff at all levels."

Conclusion

In summary, there is an overwhelming need for clear and comprehensive policies and procedures to form the basis for quality services to children. It is hoped that the experiences of the youth services managers interviewed for this article can serve as models and encouragement to others in the area of policy development.

Notes   Editorial assistance with this article was provided by William Randall Beard, Hennepin County (Minn.) Library.

1. Eleanor Estes, *Rufus M.* (New York: Harcourt Brace, 1943), 7–30.

2. Fort Vancouver Regional Library Board, *Children's Access to Library Materials: Recommendations from the Policy Committee of the Fort Vancouver Regional Library Board* (Vancouver, Wash.: Fort Vancouver Regional Library Board 1993, photocopy), i.

Bibliography

Benne, Mae. *Principles of Children's Services in Public Libraries.* Chicago: American Library Association, 1991.

Connor, Jane Gardner. *Children's Library Services Handbook.* Phoenix, Ariz.: Oryx Press, 1990.

Fort Vancouver Regional Library Board. *Children's Access to Library Materials: Recommendations from the Policy Committee of the Fort Vancouver Regional Library Board.* Vancouver, Wash.: Fort Vancouver Regional Library Board, 1993. Photocopy.

Robbins, Jane, ed., et al. *Evaluation Strategies and Techniques for Public Library Children's Services: A Sourcebook.* Madison: Univ. of Wisconsin, School of Library and Information Studies, 1990.

Rollock, Barbara T. *Public Library Services for Children*. Hamden, Conn.: Library Professional Publications, 1988.

Service to Children Committee of the Public Library Association, in collaboration with the Library Service to Children with Special Needs Committee of the Association for Library Service to Children. *Latchkey Children in the Public Library: Resources for Planners*. Chicago: American Library Association, 1988.

Simon, Anne E., ed. *Kids Welcome Here! Writing Public Library Policies That Promote Use by Young People*. Albany, N.Y.: New York Library Association, 1990.

Turner, Anne M. *It Comes with the Territory: Handling Problem Situations in Libraries*. Jefferson, N.C.: McFarland, 1993.

Van Orden, Phyllis. *Library Service to Children: A Guide to the Research, Planning, and Policy Literature*. Chicago: American Library Association, 1992.

Appendix

Participants and Survey Questions

The following librarians were interviewed for this article:

Melody Lloyd Allen, Supervisor, Young Readers Section
Rhode Island Department of State Library Services
Providence, Rhode Island

Clara Bohrer, Director
West Bloomfield Public Library
West Bloomfield, Michigan

Virginia Carlson, Children's Librarian
Pike Peak Library District
Colorado Springs, Colorado

Roseanne Cerny, Coordinator for Children's Services
Queensborough Public Library
Jamaica, New York

Gayle Cole, Coordinator of Youth Services
Stockton-San Joaquin County Public Library
Stockton, California

Joyce Dixon, Young People's Library Coordinator
Las Vegas-Clark County Library District
Las Vegas, Nevada

Leslie Edmonds, Youth Services Coordinator
Saint Louis Public Library
St. Louis, Missouri

Carole D. Fiore, Youth Services Consultant
Florida Department of State, Division of Library and Information Services
Tallahassee, Florida

Emily Holman, Chairperson Coordinator
Ocean County Public Library
Toms River, New Jersey

Shannon Lang, Coordinator of Youth Services
Mansfield-Richland County Public Library
Mansfield, Ohio

Eva-Marie Lusk, Children's Services Coordinator
Spokane Public Library
Spokane, Washington

Virginia McKee, Chief of Children's Services
Providence Public Library
Providence, Rhode Island

Alice Neve, Youth Services
   Coordinator
St. Paul Public Library
St. Paul, Minnesota

Carolyn Peterson, Coordinator of
   Children's Services (retired)
Orange County Library
Orlando, Florida

Lynne Pickens, Manager,
   Children's Department
Atlanta-Fulton Public Library
Atlanta, Georgia

Phyllis Ray, Children's Services
   Librarian
Dallas Public Library
Dallas, Texas

Debbie Sherman, Children's
   Services Coordinator
Medina County District Library
Medina, Ohio

Janice Yee, Deputy County
   Librarian
Santa Clara County Library
San Jose, California

Before the telephone conversations, these librarians received a letter describing the survey with an attachment listing the following questions:

1. Have you developed policies specific to children and youth services in areas such as behavior in the library, circulation of materials, and library card registration, storytime, etc.?
2. What incidents or series of events prompted the development of these policies?
3. What process was used to develop them and what staff was involved in the development?
4. How were they approved?
5. How were they implemented?
6. Have they been revised or do you anticipate any future revisions? Why?
7. Were children or young people involved in their development?
8. How do these policies fit in with your philosophy of service?

A final paragraph in the letter indicated interest in the stories behind the policy: how the respondents would do it differently; whether there were policies that should never have been developed; whether policies have been used in ways never intended; and, was their development different from those affecting adults.

Chapter 5

Evaluating Library Services and Programs

Virginia A. Walter

What Is Evaluation and Why Should You Do It?

Evaluation has become increasingly important in these times of resource-scarce, results-oriented government. While good managers have always had a feel for how things were going, the need to document productivity and to account for results has become a watchword for efficiency-minded government officials. In *Reinventing Government: How the Entrepreneurial Spirit Is Transforming the Public Sector,* the latest required reading for public managers, David Osborne and Ted Gaebler point out that there has been a significant shift from funding inputs to funding outcomes.[1] Policy makers want to know what kind of a bang they are going to get for their bucks, so department and agency managers are now required to anticipate results in their budget requests and to provide quantifiable measures of their achievements. These performance measures are designed to evaluate the outcomes of particular programs and services. They provide the bottom line that has traditionally been lacking in nonprofit and government organizations.

Gaebler and Osborne would probably agree with Jane Robbins, Doug Zweizig, and others at the University of Wisconsin-Madison who have been studying, developing, and applying evaluation techniques in libraries. The Wisconsin group places evaluation firmly in the context of an ongoing planning process that includes assessing needs, evaluating library resources, establishing the library role or mission, setting goals and objectives, developing strategies, implementing them, monitoring progress, evaluating progress, reviewing and updating goals, and starting the process all over again. Notice that evaluation occurs at least twice in this process. Robbins and Zweizig caution that evaluation doesn't aim to answer the question, "How good is it?" which begs the additional question, "Compared to what?" Rather, evaluation should help to answer the questions, "Are we there yet? Have we reached our objective?"[2]

In this chapter, we will be looking at the evaluation of library services and programs as a way of answering the question, "Are we there yet?"

You may have no choice; your governmental jurisdiction may already be requiring that you provide evidence of your achievement toward programmatic goals and objectives. You may be required to submit various output measures as part of your budget request justification. Certainly the need to demonstrate accountability to higher administrators and elected officials is a major reason to embark on a systematic evaluation effort. If you are involved in grant-funded projects, you are probably required to evaluate those programs. Even if nobody ever asked you for evaluation results, however, there would still be good reason to evaluate your programs and services.

As a manager, you need information on which to base your decisions. How are you going to decide to allocate your materials budget? Should you spend more on picture books this year? Should you develop your Spanish language collection? Or focus on homework assignment materials? How will you decide what array of services to offer in your department? Should you continue the preschool story hour? Offer a toddler storytime? Develop an after school program for latchkey children? How do you make decisions about staffing? Should the children's desk be staffed in the morning hours? How many librarians should be scheduled after school? You could answer all of these questions based on past practice, gut feelings, and informal rules of thumb, but an ongoing evaluation effort will provide a rational foundation on which to base your decisions. Keep in mind that the goal here is not to *prove* but to *improve*. Evaluation can provide you with information that will help you make better decisions and improve the programs and services you offer.

How Do You Evaluate Library Service to Children?

Adele Fasick has pointed out that children's librarians have sometimes resisted having to evaluate the services they provide. Some of this resistance comes from a conviction that the really important services are intangible and unquantifiable. Some is related to a resentment about having to once more justify the goodness of what we do. Some is based on the realization that there are particular difficulties involved in measuring services to children as a group.[3] Shirley Grinnell Fitzgibbons explains that young people have frequently been omitted from library planning and evaluation efforts because of problems in agreeing on definitions, problems related to the role and status of youth librarians, and the lack of consensus about measurement objectives or procedures.[4] Many of these problems and difficulties have been resolved by the publication of *Output Measures for Public Library Service to Children* by the American Library Association in 1992.[5]

Output Measures

Output Measures for Public Library Service to Children (OMPLSC) is the result of a cooperative effort between the Public Library Association (PLA) and the Association of Library Service to Children (ALSC). The goal was to tackle the definitional and procedural problems and to produce a set of output measures that clearly relate children's services to the overall role setting and planning process. This manual of standardized procedures, a companion to *Planning and Role Setting for Public Libraries* (PRSPL) and *Output Measures for Public Libraries,* second edition (OMPL), should provide you with much of what you need to know to implement an evaluation effort in your library.[6] In OMPLSC you will find an overview of the topic of measuring children's services, a discussion of some of the organizational and managerial considerations you may encounter, and general advice about collecting, interpreting, and using quantitative data. There is a summary of the eight roles that PLA has offered as a menu of service focuses that a library may choose from in defining its particular mission in a community. This is followed by specific, detailed instructions for implementing a variety of output measures that are specific to library service to children and that measure progress toward objectives that are related to the public library roles.

The output measures that are detailed in the manual are:

Library Use Measures

Children's Library Visits per Child is the average number of visits to the library by people age 14 and younger per child (14 and younger) in the community served. It measures walk-in use of the library.

Building Use by Children indicates the average number of people 14 and under who are in the library at any particular time. Together with Children's Library Visits per Child, this measure shows patterns of use.

Furniture/Equipment Use by Children measures the proportion of time, on average, that a particular type of furniture or equipment, such as preschool seating or computer terminals, is in use by people 14 and under.

Materials Use Measures

Circulation of Children's Materials per Child measures the use of children's library materials loaned for use outside the library, relative to the number of people age 14 and under in the service area.

In-Library Use of Children's Materials per Child indicates the use of children's library materials within the library, relative to the number of people age 14 and under in the community served.

Turnover Rate of Children's Materials indicates the intensity of use of the children's collection, relating the circulation of children's materials to the total size of the children's collection.

Materials Availability Measures

Children's Fill Rate is the percentage of successful searches for library materials by users age 14 and under and adults acting on behalf of children.

Homework Fill Rate is the proportion of successful searches for information or library materials for homework use by library users age 14 and under and adults acting on behalf of children.

Picture Book Fill Rate is the percentage of successful searches for picture books.

Information Services Measures

Children's Information Transactions per Child is the number of information transactions per person age 14 and under in the community served made by library users age 14 and under and adults acting on behalf of children.

Children's Information Transaction Completion Rate is the percentage of successful information transactions by persons age 14 and under and by adults acting on behalf of children.

Programming Measures

Children's Program Attendance per Child measures annual attendance at children's library programs per person age 14 and under in the community served.

Community Relations

Class Visit Rate measures visits from school classes to the library relative to the total number of school classes in the community.

Child Care Center Contact Rate is the number of contacts between the library and child care centers relative to the number of child care centers in the community.

Annual Number of Community Contacts is the total number of community contacts made by library staff resonsible for service to children during the year.[7]

Notice that OMPLSC has defined children as library users age 14 and under and has been careful to include parents and other caregivers as part of the clientele of children's services as well. Procedurally, the seasonal nature of children's services has been accounted for by directing that librarians collect data during sample periods that represent a typical week in summer and a typical week in winter and then calculating an annual figure.

When you use OMPLSC to implement evaluation activities, you will select the output measures that meet your particular needs. Rarely will a library use all of them. For each measure, the manual gives detailed instructions about how to collect the needed data, how to calculate the measure, and how to interpret the results. Suggestions are also given for following up on the results and for adapting the basic measures for particular needs. For example, Children's Program Attendance per Child can be adapted to measure Summer Reading Program Attendance per School Age Child and Circulation of Children's Materials per Child can be adapted to measure Circulation of Picture Books per Preschool Child.

The output measures are designed to provide you with quantitative data that you can use for evaluating children's services and programs. They tell you "how many" of something in relation to "how many" of something else. Sometimes, however, more qualitative data is required. You may want to know "why" or "so what?" In these instances, you can collect more subjective information through such means as interviews, open-ended questionnaires, and focus groups. OMPLSC gives you some guidance on these techniques as well. Because these output measures were designed especially for children's services in public libraries, this is probably the best place to start as you consider various evaluation strategies. The following case illustrates one use of output measures by a head of children's services.

The Case of the Young Question Seekers

A county library system was facing its first budget crisis in living memory. Tax revenues were down; mandated services were up. The county administrator announced that all county departments must prepare 5 percent and 10 percent budget reduction packages. The county librarian summoned her administrative team to a meeting to decide how to proceed. The library system had kept only the most basic statistics in the past, recording only overall annual circulation and overall annual reference count, which were the two statistics required by the state library, so there was little quantitative data on which to base the decision.

At the budget meeting, the head of Adult Services voiced the conventional wisdom of the system, that the circulation of current adult materials and the provision of basic adult reference services were the most heavily used elements of the library and therefore the aspects that could least sustain a cut. The head of Children's Services had just returned from a workshop on output measures for children's services, however, and she suggested that they collect some benchmark data before making any final decisions. The group agreed to collect data for one week, using the procedures outlined in OMPL and OMPLSC, for adult and children's reference transactions. They also agreed to collect more segmented data on circulation, breaking it down by broad class: adult fiction, adult nonfiction, adult audiovisual materials, children's audiovisual materials, children's fiction, children's nonfiction, and children's picture books.

Everybody was astonished by the results except the head of Children's Services. This is a system with a central library and ten branches. When the results were tallied, the overall children's reference count (questions asked by children and their caregivers) was 60 percent of the total. At all ten branches, children's questions accounted for at least 75 percent of the total, with only central library having more than 50 percent of its queries originating with adults. Picture books accounted for 23 percent of the total circulation. Altogether, children's library materials accounted for 62 percent of the total circulation.

The county librarian drew up reduction packages that focused on adult reference and adult periodicals and made a special request for augmentation of the children's picture book collection. She also conducted a needs assessment and formal planning process, which resulted in the library adopting Preschoolers' Door to Learning, Formal Support to Education, and Independent Learning Center as their three primary roles. Staff devised a systematic implementation of appropriate output measures to monitor their progress in fulfilling those roles.

Total Quality Management

Many public libraries, particularly those that have adopted the planning and role setting process developed by the Public Library Association's Public Library Development Project, find that output measures satisfy their needs for ongoing evaluation of programs and services. Sometimes, however, local circumstances may suggest another approach. Some local governments, for example, have embraced Total Quality Management (TQM) as their primary managerial strategy. TQM suggests a somewhat different approach to ongoing evaluation.

Developed originally in the 1930s by an American industrial engineer, W. Edwards Deming, TQM is an overall approach to management that stresses the continuous improvement of an organization's processes, resulting in high-quality products and services. It places a high premium on customer satisfaction and worker participation in decisions that affect work quality.[8] TQM has a long history, particularly in Japan, where Deming first instituted it in 1950 and where it may have contributed to the remarkable post-war industrial renaissance of that country.

One aspect of the Japanese implementation of TQM was reintroduced into the United States in the 1970s in the form of quality circles. In quality circles, small groups of workers assigned to the same tasks meet regularly to identify and solve problems at their outset, to monitor the work processes and output for which they are responsible, and to improve the quality of their work. It is a form of ongoing evaluation by the people responsible for doing the work. In a library, for example, the librarians in the reference department could form a quality circle. They would be responsible for developing customer-driven feedback mechanisms that would enable them to monitor the quality of their work on an ongoing basis, and for correcting problems as they occurred. They would aim at continuous improvement of the quality of their service.

More recent manifestations of TQM have aimed at a more comprehensive approach than the institution of quality circles. There is an effort to embrace an overall organizational culture devoted to quality improvement. While not all TQM organizations follow all of Deming's fourteen points, they do try to emphasize the importance of meeting customer requirements for quality, to focus on process, to involve workers, to implement feedback mechanisms, and to make decisions based on fact. Statistical methods become important in developing the feedback mechanisms that produce the facts on which decisions are based.

While Deming's approach to quality control was developed originally for manufacturing operations, it has been applied to service, nonprofit, and public sector organizations with some success. Warren H. Schmidt and Jerome P. Finnigan document examples of TQM in such varied settings as the Department of Defense; the state of Arkansas; the cities of Madison, Wisconsin and Austin, Texas; Oregon State University; and the Sacramento County School District.[9] They acknowledge that TQM is often more difficult to implement in government organizations than in private organizations because of their multiple constituencies and political constraints, but maintain that TQM nevertheless has much to offer beleaguered public agencies. Writing in *Public Administration Review,* James E. Swiss agrees, arguing for a modified version of TQM that stresses client feedback, performance monitoring, continuous improvement, and worker participation.[10] Thomas Shaughnessy has suggested some ways that TQM could be applied to academic libraries, using quantitative benchmarks such as waiting time and title availability to monitor critical variables that affect client satisfaction with the service.[11]

Output measures could be easily adapted to serve as the quantitative benchmarks needed to monitor continuous improvement in a TQM program. All you would need to add is a mechanism for regular staff input in problem solving and a self-conscious focus on customer satisfaction. See how one senior children's librarian used TQM to improve service in "The Case of the Missing Preschoolers."

The Case of the Missing Preschoolers

A suburban library had a long-established tradition of wildly successful preschool story hours. The senior children's librarian and her two assistants normally conducted four six-week story hour series each year. There were three sessions of each series, held on three different weekday mornings. Attendance at each session was limited to twenty-five children between the ages of three and five, with required preregistration. There was always a waiting list, and children on the waiting list were given the first opportunity to sign up for the next series.

This approach, which had been successful for the last ten years, began suddenly to show signs of diminishing returns. The fall series filled up, but there was no waiting list. The winter series had empty slots for the Monday session, and the spring series had empty slots on all days. Before announcing the summer series, the senior children's librarian asked for a meeting with the city librarian. The city librarian had just been sent to a training session on Total Quality Management, which the city manager was urging on all city departments. He suggested that they look at the declining preschool story hour attendance in the context of TQM.

The senior children's librarian accordingly met with her two assistants immediately to try to assess the problem as they saw it. At first they confessed bewilderment, but as they talked more, one of the women pointed out that lately more of the children who came to story hour were brought by baby-sitters. Another pointed out that there seemed to be more little brothers and sisters who were too young for story hour. They all agreed that they needed to get some feedback from the parents and caregivers who were still bringing children. They devised a parent survey and distributed it at the next story hour. They asked questions about general satisfaction with the story hour and asked for suggestions for improvement. They also called in a colleague from a nearby library who conducted a series of focus groups with parents still attending story hour and with some who had dropped out.

What they learned was that many mothers had returned to work and could no longer bring their children to preschool story hour. Some had nannies who could still bring the children to the library, but most had put their children in day care arrangements. Many of those mothers said they would welcome an opportunity to share a family outing to the library if it were at an appropriate time. Another group of mothers said that the birth of younger brothers and sisters made preschool story hour for three to five year olds increasingly less relevant. They were interested in services for their younger children.

The staff of the children's department responded by eliminating two sessions of preschool story hour and instituting a new toddler time for two year olds and an early evening family story hour aimed at working parents and their children. The city librarian agreed to hire extra temporary librarians to conduct extra sessions for any of these programs when the waiting list reaches fifteen. For now, all three programs are well-attended, and parent satisfaction as recorded on evaluation cards is high. Two additional sessions of toddler time have been added. The children's librarians continue to monitor parent satisfaction with all three programs and to meet regularly to discuss how to improve the quality of each.

Program Evaluation

Program evaluation differs from the kind of overall performance evaluation we have been discussing primarily in its scope. Program evaluation looks at how specific programs are meeting the specific objectives that have been established for them. It is often built into grant-funded projects, for example, in order to determine that the project implementation complies with its original goals. Often funding agencies want to know whether demonstration or pilot projects should be implemented more widely. There may be efforts to determine outcomes or impacts of the program on participants, as well as the objective results, or outputs. This usually requires a multidimensional evaluation, using more than one method of feedback.

Program evaluation usually takes one of two forms. Summative evaluation is the final summary of the effectiveness of a program. Formative evaluation, on the other hand, takes place throughout the life of a project. The evaluator functions as a kind of consultant, helping to identify problems and develop solutions as the program is implemented.[12] Either or both types of evaluation may be specifically required by a funding agency, and the agency may prefer that an outside evaluator do the work rather than the staff who are implementing the program.

Once again, output measures may provide a starting point for thinking about techniques that can be used to demonstrate achievement of specific program objectives. As you develop grant proposals, look at the manual to see if there are measures that can be adapted. A strong grant proposal will have its evaluation strategy integrated with its objectives and action plan. "The Case of Grandparents and Books" shows how program evaluation was implemented in one grant-funded project.

The Case of Grandparents and Books

A large urban library system successfully applied for a Library Services and Construction Act (LSCA) grant through their state library to start a demonstration project to train older adult volunteers to share books and stories with children, using read-aloud, flannel board, and puppet techniques. The older adults then became library "grandparents" who worked with children informally after school as part of the library's overall service program.

As is customary with grant-funded projects, the library had established quantitative goals for Grandparents and Books. During the first year, they planned to reach 300 adults and 900 children in the three branches that had been designated pilot sites. Rigorous statistical counts were maintained of the number of volunteers and the number of hours they contributed and the number of children who participated. At the end of the year, they discovered that they had reached far fewer adults than targeted—only 125 instead of the anticipated 300. They had also reached far more children than expected—5,500 instead of the anticipated 900. The smaller cadre of volunteer grandparents turned out to be unusually productive, putting in far more hours than anyone had expected.

With these provocative statistics and with anecdotal evidence from staff that the program seemed to be succeeding in somewhat surprising ways, the state library agreed to fund the program for another year with the proviso that the program be evaluated to determine the impact that the program had on both grandparents and children. The funding agency wanted outcome measures as well as output measures.

An evaluator from the local university was hired who conducted a written survey of all volunteers, designed to elicit their satisfaction with various elements of the program. The evaluator also conducted focus groups with representative grandparents and child participants. The results indicated that participating in Grandparents and Books fulfilled particular social and personal needs of the volunteers, enabling them to continue to feel useful in their communities and to have meaningful relationships with children. The children also expressed positive feelings about the cross-generational aspects of the program as well as general satisfaction with having someone pay attention to them on a one-to-one basis.

These qualitative findings about the outcomes of the Grandparents and Books program, combined with the continued productivity of the volunteers as documented in the statistical reporting, convinced the state library to extend the program throughout the state with start-up funding over the next three years.

Conclusion

Youth services in public libraries have always been characterized by good intentions. Like motherhood and apple pie, the combination of children and books seemed to be core American values. Motherhood has changed a lot in recent years, however, as social changes and medical advances have introduced such phenomena as extra-uterine insemination and surrogate mothers. Even apple pie isn't what it used to be, as dieticians create new low-fat, low-sugar versions of the all-American dessert. Children and books don't come together as easily and naturally as they used to either, in this age of lowered reading scores, Nintendo, and MTV. Youth services librarians need all the political and managerial savvy they can get to be effective advocates for children's rights to read and to know as we move into the twenty-first century. Evaluation is an essential part of your professional tool kit, helping you to judge your effectiveness as you implement your good intentions.

Notes

1. David Osborne and Ted Gaebler, *Reinventing Government: How the Entrepreneurial Spirit Is Transforming the Public Sector* (Reading, Mass.: Addison-Wesley, 1992), 138ff.

2. Jane Robbins and Douglas L. Zweizig, *Are We There Yet?* (Madison: Univ. of Wisconsin, School of Library and Information Studies, 1988), 1–7.

3. Adele Fasick, "Research and Measurement in Library Services to Children," in *Evaluation Strategies and Techniques for Public Library Children's Services: A Sourcebook,* by Jane Robbins et al. (Madison: Univ. of Wisconsin, School of Library and Information Studies, 1990), 19–30.

4. Shirley Grinnell Fitzgibbons, "Accountability of Library Services for Youth: A Planning, Measurement, and Evaluation Model," in *Library Performance, Accountability, and Responsiveness: Essays in Honor of Ernest R. Deprospo,* ed. Charles C. Curran and F. William Summers (Norwood, N.J.: Ablex, 1990), 65–84.

5. Virginia A. Walter, *Output Measures for Public Library Service to Children: A Manual of Standardized Procedures* (Chicago: American Library Association, 1992).

6. Charles R. McClure et al., *Planning and Role Setting for Public Libraries: A Manual of Options and Procedures* (Chicago: American Library Association, 1987) and Nancy A. Van House et al., *Output Measures for Public Libraries: A Manual of Standardized Procedures,* 2d ed. (Chicago: American Library Association, 1987). These are both products of the Public Library Development Project sponsored by the Public Library Association.

7. Walter, *Output Measures,* 2.

8. Marshall Sashkin and Kenneth J. Kiser, *Putting Total Quality Management to Work* (San Francisco: Berrett-Koehler, 1993), 39.

9. Warren H. Schmidt and Jerome P. Finnigan, *The Race without a Finish Line: America's Quest for Total Quality* (San Francisco: Jossey-Bass, 1992).

10. James E. Swiss, "Adapting Total Quality Management (TQM) to Government," *Public Administration Review* 52 (July-August 1992):356–61.

11. Thomas W. Shaughnessy, "Benchmarking, Total Quality Management, and Libraries," *Library Administration and Management* 7 (Winter 1993):7–12.

12. Carol Taylor Fitz-Gibbon and Lynn Lyons Morris, *How to Design a Program Evaluation* (Newbury Park, Calif.: Sage, 1987), 11.

Bibliography

Baker, Sharon L. and F. Wilfrid Lancaster. *The Measurement and Evaluation of Library Services,* 2d ed. Arlington, Va.: Information Resources Press, 1991.

Berk, Richard A. and Peter H. Rossi. *Thinking about Program Evaluation.* Newbury Park, Calif.: Sage, 1990.

Chelton, Mary K. "Evaluation of Children's Services." *Library Trends* 37 (Winter 1987):463–84.

Childers, Thomas A. and Nancy A. Van House. *What's Good? Describing Your Public Library's Effectiveness.* Chicago: American Library Association, 1993.

Curran, Charles C. and F. William Summers. *Library Performance, Accountability, and Responsiveness: Essays in Honor of Ernest R. DeProspo.* Norwood, N.J.: Ablex, 1990.

Fitz-Gibbon, Carol Taylor and Lynn Lyons Morris. *How to Design a Program Evaluation.* Newbury Park, Calif.: Sage, 1987.

Franklin, Barbara and Margaret Hamil. "Youth Services Evaluation in the Small Library: A Case Study." *Public Libraries* 31 (September-October 1992):278–83.

Garland, Kathleen. "Children's Services Statistics: A Study of State Agency and Individual Library Activity." *Public Libraries* 31 (November-December 1992):351–55.

Gault, Robin R. "Performance Measures for Evaluating Public Library Children's Services." *Public Libraries* 23 (Winter 1984):134–37.

Greenbaum, Thomas L. *The Practical Handbook and Guide to Focus Group Research.* Lexington, Mass.: Lexington Books, 1988.

Herman, Joan L. et al. *Evaluator's Handbook.* Newbury Park, Calif.: Sage, 1987.

Krueger, Richard A. *Focus Groups: A Practical Guide for Applied Research.* Newbury Park, Calif.: Sage, 1988.

McClure, Charles R., Douglas L. Zweizig, Nancy A. Van House, and Mary Jo Lynch. "Output Measures: Myths, Realities, and Prospects." *Public Libraries* 25 (September 1986):49–52.

Mielke, Laurie R. "Sermon on the Amount: Costing Out Children's Services." *Public Libraries* 30 (September-October 1991):279–82.

Morris, Lynn Lyons et al. *How to Communicate Evaluation Findings.* Newbury Park, Calif.: Sage, 1987.

Robbins, Jane et al. *Evaluation Strategies and Techniques for Public Library Children's Services: A Sourcebook.* Madison: Univ. of Wisconsin, School of Library and Information Studies, 1990.

Sashkin, Marshall and Kenneth J. Kiser. *Putting Total Quality Management to Work.* San Francisco: Berrett-Koehler, 1993.

Schmidt, Warren H. and Jerome P. Finnigan. *The Race without a Finish Line: America's Quest for Total Quality.* San Francisco: Jossey-Bass, 1992.

Shaughnessy, Thomas W. "Assessing Library Effectiveness." *Journal of Library Administration* 12 (1990):1–8.

Shaughnessy, Thomas W. "Benchmarking, Total Quality Management, and Libraries." *Library Administration and Management* 7 (Winter 1993):7–12.

Swiss, James E. "Adapting Total Quality Management (TQM) to Government." *Public Administration Review* 52 (July-August 1992):356–61.

Van House, Nancy A. and Thomas Childers. "Prospects for Public Library Evaluation." *Public Libraries* 30 (September-October 1991):274–78.

Van House, Nancy A., Mary Jo Lynch, Charles R. McClure, Douglas L. Zweizig, and Eleanor Jo Rodger. *Output Measures for Public Libraries: A Manual of Standardized Procedures,* 2d ed. Chicago: American Library Association, 1987.

Walter, Virginia A. *Output Measures for Public Library Service to Children: A Manual of Standardized Procedures.* Chicago: American Library Association, 1992.

Weech, Terry L. "Validity and Comparability of Public Library Data: A Commentary on the Output Measures for Public Libraries." *Public Library Quarterly* 8 (1988):7–18.

Wholey, Joseph. *Evaluation and Effective Public Management.* Boston: Little, Brown, 1983.

Wholey, Joseph S. et al. *Improving Government Performance: Evaluation Strategies for Strengthening Public Agencies and Programs.* San Francisco: Jossey-Bass, 1989.

Wilson, Cynthia M. "Output Measures Identify Problems and Solutions for Middle Schoolers." *Public Libraries* 29 (January-February 1990):19–22.

Wiseman, Mary Jane. "Research and the Evaluation of Children's Services." *Journal of Youth Services in Libraries* 3 (Summer 1990):321–23.

Chapter 6

Job Descriptions

Yvette Johnson

Now is the time to check through your departmental job descriptions. If you haven't revised them since the Americans with Disabilities Act (ADA) of 1990, then they definitely need your attention. At best your job descriptions are probably too vague, and at worst they may violate the new law.

Job descriptions are important for a number of reasons. They not only clarify the responsibilities of each position in the library and delineate the relationship between positions, but they also serve as the basis for the performance evaluation.[1] Well-written descriptions may also serve as protection against litigation.[2]

Before undertaking a revision of job descriptions, there are preliminary steps to be taken. First of all, your library should conduct a job audit or job analysis. Second, from this job audit information, your library should develop a classification of its positions. Ideally, it is the information gleaned from these exercises that will provide the focus for the revision of your job descriptions.

The job audit is an objective look at the responsibilities of each position in the library. It provides both a linkage between those jobs across all departments that have like responsibilities and an opportunity to classify them. The implications for youth services are clear. There is a feeling among some youth services librarians that their jobs are not compensated at the same level as those librarians who work in adult services. The exercises of job audit and position classifications will reveal any such inequity.

In 1990 the Glenview Public Library underwent a job audit. The director, with the advice of an outside consultant, developed a three-page form that was to be filled out by each employee (*see* figure 1). Before it was ever handed out, he wisely prepared the staff. Concern dissipated when he made it clear that it was the *position* that was to be analyzed, and not the employee holding it. His memo explained what was to be done, when, and why. The *why* of the exercise was of greatest concern to all staff. Some wondered if their positions might be in jeopardy. Again, it was clarified

Glenview Public Library
Position Description

Date: _____

Name _____

Job Title _____   Full time? (Yes/No)

Department _____

Title of supervisor _____

Job duties performed regularly: list in order of importance

Duty	Percent of time devoted to duty	Supervisor's comments
1. _____	_____	_____
2. _____	_____	_____
3. _____	_____	_____
4. _____	_____	_____
5. _____	_____	_____
6. _____	_____	_____
7. _____	_____	_____
8. _____	_____	_____
9. _____	_____	_____
10. _____	_____	_____

Other duties performed, indicate frequency (use an additional sheet, if necessary):

What machines or equipment is the jobholder responsible for operating?

What are the working conditions? List such items as public contact, outside work, lifting, pushing, or exposure to heat and noise.

Contacts: indicate those you must contact to carry out your job:

a. Internal to library

b. External to library

FIGURE 1.   Glenview (Ill.) Public Library Position Description. Reprinted with permission

Positions directly supervised	Number
_____	_____
_____	_____
_____	_____

(If there are more, please list on a separate sheet and attach.)

Positions indirectly supervised

_____	_____
_____	_____

(If there are more, please list on a separate sheet and attach.)

To be filled out by supervisor:

How often is this position given (circle one for each category):

a. Supervision: *Constantly*   *Frequently*   *Infrequently*   *Almost never*

b. Instructions: *Constantly*   *Frequently*   *Infrequently*   *Almost never*

c. Discretionary
   authority: *Constantly*   *Frequently*   *Infrequently*   *Almost never*

d. Authority over
   others: *Constantly*   *Frequently*   *Infrequently*   *Almost never*

At what stage is the jobholder's work reviewed by the supervisor?

If the jobholder made a serious mistake or error in performing the required duties, what would the impact be to library service?

Minimum job requirements:

a. Equivalent education level required:

b. Experience required:

c. Knowledge required:

d. Professional degrees or licenses required:

Supervisor's
Name and title _____ Date _____

Review by Executive Librarian _____ Date _____

that no job was in danger, and no reductions in pay would result. Instead, the intent was to develop a new classification system for all library jobs in order to establish an equitable system of compensation.[3]

This position description form asked each employee to list ten duties by order of importance, followed by the percentage of time devoted to each duty. Several questions ascertained the working conditions peculiar to that position, while others focused on the amount of supervision, independent judgment, and networking required of the position. All employees then gave the completed form to their supervisors for a reality check. The supervisor noted any differences in his or her perception about the duties and percentage of time devoted to them.

Part of the form was to be filled out by the supervisor alone. Questions here would help determine the amount of responsibility for other staff and finances held by the position, as well as its relative autonomy. Crucial to the maintenance of the objectivity of the entire exercise was that a copy of the completed form was returned to each employee after it had been reviewed by the director.

Some authorities consider that conducting personal interviews with each employee should be part of the job analysis process.[4] As it turned out, even though this aspect was not part of the formal process at the Glenview Public Library, the fact that these forms were shared between each employee and his or her supervisor gave rise to much informal dialogue and discussion.

The next step involved the director and the outside consultant, who weighed the positions in order to arrive at a more equitable job classification system for the library. In fall 1991 this was unveiled, much to the delight of staff. Where in the past there had been only one level of paraprofessional, for instance, the job analysis made clear that there should be more. The new classification system created three levels of paraprofessionals for the library.

Figure 2 shows the new positions at the library, all of which were created out of the old ones. That year staff not only received regular salary increases, many also received adjustments that recognized their new classification up to a higher level in the organization. For all staff it was gratifying to know that the library board and executive director would act more fairly to recompense the differences between work load and responsibility among existing positions.

You will note that there is no departmentally related discrepancy in this classification system. Youth services personnel at one level are compensated the same as their counterparts in adult services.

Although unfairness was never an issue at Glenview, the director avoided even a hint of its perception by hiring an outside personnel consultant to interpret the level of responsibility for each position. Unless such a disinterested person is involved, there is always the danger that a position from one department could be classified as Librarian II, for example, while a similarly responsible one from another department is classified as Librarian I.

No matter how unbiased the director might try to be, he or she could unwittingly determine the hierarchical value of a position by the caliber

Glenview Public Library
New Classification System
Basic Elements of Job Classes
October, 1991

This material describes the basic elements of each class in the new classification system. Being very brief, these "snapshots" are not job descriptions. In many classes, there are several distinct jobs which are similar in a number of broadly defined ways: amount of expertise, supervisory authority, education, independence, public contact, and experience required.

Library Group (Grade number follows an "L"):

Grade: 100   Class: Executive Librarian
   Responsibility for all library operations. ALA/MLS required. More than five years' administrative experience required. Reports directly to Board of Trustees.

Grade: 95   Class: Assistant Librarian
   Responsibility for operations of Adult Services Department. Responsibility, in Executive Librarian's absence, for library operations. Member of management team. ALA/MLS required. More than three years' administrative experience required.

Grade: 90   Class: Department Head
   Responsibility for operations of a library department. Member of management team. ALA/MLS required. Administrative experience and related technical experience required.

Grade: 85   Class: Librarian III
   Responsibility for operation of a specialized program within a department, supervisory responsibility, direct public service. ALA/MLS required. Appropriate technical and professional experience required.

Grade: 80   Class: Librarian II
   Responsibility for specialized projects, areas of service, direct public service. ALA/MLS required. Appropriate technical and professional experience required.

Grade: 75   Class: Librarian I
   Direct public service, some projects as assigned. ALA/MLS required.

Grade: 70   Class: Circulation Chief
   Responsibility for operations of the Circulation Department, computerized circulation routines, direct public service. Member of the management team. BA or BS or equivalent required. Managerial and technical experience required.

Grade: 60   Class: Paraprofessional III
   Responsibility for specialized project or projects, some supervisory responsibility, direct public service. BA or BS or equivalent required. Appropriate library or technical experience required. Supervisory experience required depending on particular job requirements.

Grade: 55   Class: Paraprofessional II
   Responsibility for special projects, direct public service. BA or BS or equivalent required. Appropriate library or technical experience required.

Grade: 50   Class: Paraprofessional I
   Direct public service. BA or BS or equivalent required.

Continued

FIGURE 2.   Glenview Public Library, New Classification System

Grade: 45   Class: Clerk Supervisor
Responsibility for operations of specific clerical areas, including supervision of clerical staff. May include direct public service. H.S. diploma required. Appropriate work, technical, and supervisory experience required.

Grade: 40   Class: Clerk III
Responsibility for specific areas. Some lead-worker responsibilities. May include direct public service. H.S. diploma required. Appropriate work or technical experience required.

Grade: 40   Class: Monitor
Responsibility for maintaining order, enforcing library policy, interpreting library rules. Direct public contact. Independent judgment. H.S. diploma required. Relevant experience required.

Grade: 35   Class: Clerk II
Responsibility for assigned routines, and may include direct public service. H.S. diploma required. Appropriate work or technical experience required.

Grade: 30   Class: Clerk I
Responsibility for assigned routines. May include direct public service. H.S. diploma required.

Grade: 20   Class: Shelver II
Responsibility for assigned shelving routines, some special assignments, lead-worker duties. Basic work abilities required. Appropriate library experience required.

Grade: 15   Class: Shelver I
Responsibility for assigned shelving routines. Basic work abilities required. Appropriate library experience required.

Grade: 10   Class: Page
Responsibility for assigned routines. Basic work abilities required.

Administrative Group (grade number follows an "A"):

Grade: 65   Class: Office Manager
Responsibility for operations of the Business Office, supervision, and contact with the Board of Trustees. Member of the management team. H.S. Diploma, appropriate additional education, and relevant technical and supervisory experience required.

Grade: 65   Class: Public Information Officer
Responsibility for the library's public information program, some supervision. Member of the management team. B.A. or B.S. and relevant experience required.

Grade: 60   Class: Building Supervisor
Responsibility for maintenance and operations of the physical plant. Member of the management team. H.S. Diploma and relevant technical and supervisory experience required.

Grade: 50   Class: Graphic Artist
Responsibility for execution of art work in support of library programs. Relevant experience and skills required.

Grade: 40   Class: Assistant Office Manager
Responsibility for assigned tasks and special projects in the Business Office. H.S. Diploma and relevant work experience required.

Grade: 25   Class: Custodian
Responsibility for assigned tasks. Relevant experience required.

FIGURE 2.   Glenview Public Library, New Classification System—*Continued*

of the person currently holding it, or by the age level of the clientele served by said position. Even a small library with few positions should find the funds to consult with outside expertise.

After the job audit has clarified the level of responsibility of the position, and the classification system has defined exactly where the position fits in the library hierarchy and its range of remuneration, it is time to draw up a job description.

It should be noted that parlance varies among the experts. One source uses job description and position description interchangeably.[5] Another makes very specific differences between the two phrases. Stueart and Sullivan refer to a job description as "a group of positions that normally involve the same level of . . . skills, knowledge, and abilities . . . SKA's. Individuals holding that job category may be scattered throughout the library organization. . . . [like all] . . . Librarian I's or whatever the designation might be."[6] They reserve the term position description to describe one single job within the organization.

For simplicity's sake we will use the phrase *job description* in the discussion below to refer to a single specific position in the library.

According to Wendover, a job description should have the following basics:

1. A brief overview of the position that includes its role within the organization.
2. A list of duties.
3. An explanation of the reporting structure. Who supervises this position? Who is supervised by it?
4. Necessary qualifications for the position.
5. Training necessary.
6. Method of performance appraisal.[7]

Wendover recommends that compensation information not be included in the job description since it changes often. Rather a separate salary and compensation schedule should be developed.[8] Wendover's list of basics for a job description is standard information. It was written before the ADA went into effect. Libraries used this organization or something similar for years, but now new legislation makes such a general format outdated, if not unwise from a legal point of view.

The recent passage of the ADA demands that we take a new look at our job descriptions. Rachel Blegen, a human resources consultant and formerly personnel manager for Northwestern University in Illinois, feels that this act will impose a healthy discipline on the preparation of job descriptions. She said, "The ADA forces us to look carefully at what is really required to do a job. Job descriptions must become more defined. The wording will have to be more specific. In the past people with disabilities who could have done the essentials of a job were routinely denied the employment opportunity. This legislation will help to eradicate that inequity."[9]

Title I of the Americans with Disabilities Act requires the "fair treatment of qualified individuals with disabilities . . . able to perform the essential functions of a job, with or without a reasonable accommodation. To determine if a person is qualified . . . the employer must identify, in advance, the essential and non-essential functions of the job, and then determine whether the individual can perform them."[10]

Although the ADA does not require employers to have written job descriptions, it is strongly recommended here. An accurately written job description can be protection against litigation, because one of the factors that is used to determine if a particular work function is essential is that it is so stated in a written job description. On the other hand, if a job responsibility is listed as essential in a job description, then it must truly be so. Otherwise, there is no protection against litigation. A written job description may state that an employee performs a certain essential function. The job description will be evidence that the function is essential, but if individuals currently performing the job do not in fact perform this function, or perform it very infrequently, a review of the actual work performed will be more relevant evidence than the job description.[11]

The job description does not have to limit itself to a listing of only the essential functions in order to comply with the ADA. "A job typically includes both essential and non-essential, or marginal, functions. If the essential functions are the musts, the non-essential functions are the also to be dones. Examples of marginal functions would include . . . driving for a stockbroker who only makes sales in an office."[12]

It behooves us to consider each position in our department as to its essential and nonessential or additional functions. If you have a staff person whose main responsibility is regularly scheduled outreach to the schools, then it might be essential that he or she have a driver's license and car. On the other hand, if the person actually visits the schools only once or twice a year, then such a requirement might be considered unfair. In that case, reasonable accommodation dictates that other arrangements could be made. Thus a disabled person who does not have a driver's license might still very successfully be able to perform all the really essential functions of this job.

The size of the staff will have a bearing on which duties are essential and which are additional. If your department is a one- or two-person operation, then there is little room to maneuver in order to reassign or rearrange duties. In effect, each of you is doing it all. Therefore, all of your duties could be considered essential.[13]

Blegen pointed out that time and litigation will be required before we understand in a concrete way what the law means by the phrases essential functions and reasonable accommodation, but that what should be done now is to review existing job descriptions and revise them according to our best understanding of compliance with the new law.[14]

Besides this latest civil rights legislation, it would be useful to refresh one's memory about older federal laws that govern language and practice for such personnel communications. Both Wendover and Stueart and Sullivan include extensive information on the Civil Rights Act of 1964 and many subjects that are unlawful to discuss during an interview or to ask on an employment form.[15]

Blegen had other advice about job descriptions. "Too many job descriptions put technical skills first, as the paramount duty. For a public service agency like the library, the most important skill should be the *people* skills, and they should be stated first." She continued, "It is a useful exercise for a nonprofit agency to think about the *cost* of actions. For instance, what is the cost of a complaint to an operation? Factor it out relative to a supervisor's time and energy. It could also have longer-lasting impact in terms of lost goodwill or even funding. Or the cost of a brusque employee can remain hidden, but be no less real. For instance, a young child can carry with him an apprehension, even a fear, of the library and librarians."[16]

A discussion of job descriptions for youth services should at least mention the thorny issue of what constitutes professional versus paraprofessional duties. This is certainly not unique to youth services, but instead cuts across all specialties of librarianship. (For an interesting study of this general topic, see "The Future of Public Library Support Staff" by Richard Rubin.)

Although there is much room for differing opinions about which duties should be professional and which paraprofessional, perhaps we can make some generalizations that can be agreed upon. It is probably accurate, as Blegen stated during discussion, that the duties of the professional and the paraprofessional overlap about 70 percent of the time, but it is that 30 percent of the professional's time that should constitute the difference. She added that what should be required of professionals is depth of knowledge and willingness to take on higher levels of responsibility. Professionals should have the obligation always to consider the big picture, and it should be so identified in the professional job description. There should be some difference between the job descriptions for these two employee positions.[17]

Very useful as resources for the development of job descriptions for professional youth librarians are the two competency documents published by ALA: *Competencies for Librarians Serving Children in Public Libraries* (ALSC/ALA, 1989) and *Young Adults Deserve the Best: Competencies for Librarians Serving Youth* (YASD/ALA, 1989.) They are thoughtfully written pamphlets about the specific skills, knowledges, and abilities that go into the specialty of the youth services librarian. In fact the task force that recently completed a revision of the guidelines governing youth services in Illinois so stated in its document: "The Competencies documents published by the Youth divisions of ALA are appropriate resources for the preparation of professional job descriptions for Youth Librarians in Illinois public libraries."[18]

It is daunting to consider the amount of work that will go into a complete revision of your library's job descriptions. A job analysis and job classification process should precede the revisions, and the job descriptions themselves should be rewritten with a knowledge of the Americans with Disabilities Act and other legislation. The entire library will need to be involved at some level. The administration must set up the structure for the work to be done, and the department heads should clearly understand its importance. All must work together in order to reach the goal of equity within the organization.

The time to start is now, while you have all your positions filled. Go into the files and take a look at the job description under which you were hired some years ago. That dusty document which no longer defines your work may be all the motivation you need to show this article to your boss and get the ball rolling in your library.

Notes

1. Robert D. Stueart and Maureen Sullivan, *Performance Analysis and Appraisal: A How-to-Do-It Manual for Librarians* (New York: Neal-Schuman, 1991), 9–11.

2. Robert W. Wendover, *Smart Hiring: The Complete Guide for Recruiting Employees* (Englewood, Colo.: Management Staff Press, 1989), 5.

3. Glenview Public Library, Administration to Library Staff, memorandum, June 18, 1990 (Glenview, Ill.: Glenview Public Library).

4. Sheila Creth and Frederick Duda, eds., *Personnel Administration in Libraries,* 2d ed. (New York: Neal-Schuman, 1989), 75, and Stueart and Sullivan, *Performance Analysis,* 8.

5. Barbara I. Dewey, *Library Jobs: How to Fill Them, How to Find Them* (Phoenix, Ariz.: Oryx Press, 1987), 28.

6. Stueart and Sullivan, *Performance Analysis,* 5.

7. Wendover, *Smart Hiring,* 26–27.

8. Ibid., 27–28.

9. Rachel Blegen, interview by author, Evanston, Ill., June 15, 1993.

10. *Americans with Disabilities Act: ADA Compliance Guide* (Washington, D.C.: Thompson Publishing Group, 1990), Tab 300, p. 25.

11. Ibid., 161.

12. Ibid., 27.

13. Ibid.

14. Rachel Blegen, interview.

15. Wendover, *Smart Hiring,* 9–16, and Stueart and Sullivan, *Performance Analysis,* 25–34.

16. Rachel Blegen, interview.

17. Ibid.

18. *Managing Change: Directions for Youth Services in Illinois Public Libraries* (Chicago: Illinois Library Association), 20.

Bibliography

Americans with Disabilities Act: ADA Compliance Guide. Washington, D.C.: Thompson Publishing Group, 1990.

Americans with Disabilities Act Handbook, Equal Employment Opportunity Commission and the U.S. Department of Justice (EEOC-BK-18), 1991.

The Americans with Disabilities Act: Your Employment Rights as an Individual with a Disability. U.S. Equal Employment Opportunity Commission (EEOC-BK-18), 1991.

Blegen, Rachel. Interview by author. Evanston, Ill. June 15, 1993.

Competencies for Librarians Serving Children in Public Libraries. Chicago: ALSC/ American Library Association, 1989.

Creth, Sheila and Frederick Duda, eds. *Personnel Administration in Libraries,* 2d ed. New York: Neal-Schuman, 1989.

Dewey, Barbara I. *Library Jobs: How to Fill Them, How to Find Them.* Phoenix, Ariz.: Oryx Press, 1987.

Glenview Public Library Administration to Library Staff, memorandums, June 18, 1990 and October 1991. Glenview, Ill.: Glenview Public Library.

Managing Change: Directions for Youth Services in Illinois Public Libraries. Chicago: Illinois Library Association, 1993.

Rubin, Richard. "The Future of Public Library Support Staff." *Public Library Quarterly* 12, no. 1 (1992):17–29.

Stueart, Robert D. and Maureen Sullivan. *Performance Analysis and Appraisal: A How-to-Do-It Manual for Librarians.* New York: Neal-Schuman, 1991.

Wendover, Robert W. *Smart Hiring. The Complete Guide for Recruiting Employees.* Englewood, Colo.: Management Staff Press, 1989.

Young Adults Deserve the Best: Competencies for Librarians Serving Youth. Chicago: YASD/American Library Association, 1989. Reprint from *School Library Journal,* 1982.

Chapter 7

Recruiting and Retaining Youth Services Librarians

Maria B. Salvadore

Libraries invest heavily in staff. On average, more than 50 percent of public libraries' annual expenditures are devoted to salaries.[1] If defined only in fiscal terms, human resources literally are a library's greatest asset. The notion of investment in staff by libraries, however, goes well beyond dollars. Libraries are investments in people—those served and those who serve. The discussion that follows will focus on practical aspects of recruiting and retaining youth services librarians at the local, regional, and national level. It should be noted that in this discussion, a master's degree is considered necessary to qualify as a professional librarian. The master's degree represents a requisite level of education for entry into the field in this capacity. The specifics of the professional position have been outlined by the American Library Association (ALA). Additionally, since the process of interviewing can be considered recruitment as well as an assessment device, interviewing will also be covered briefly.

Youth Services for the Future: Recruitment

The first thing to note when addressing the issue of recruiting is that the field of candidates is likely to be small. While library use has increased, the number of graduates from ALA-accredited programs has declined.[2] The ALA Special Committee on Library School Closings reported that there were 6,336 graduates from library education programs in 1973, while only 3,625 graduated in 1992, a decrease of 43 percent.[3] The most often cited shortages have been in youth services.[4] What can be done to encourage more people to seriously explore library work with children and youth? One strategy for recruiters is to enlarge their field of candidates by working with other community agencies to find (or inform) likely candidates. The Task Force on Youth Development and Community Programs, convened by the Carnegie Council on Adolescent Development, suggests that networking within the community provides important information to potential employees about work with youth as a career choice.[5] This information may be targeted to individuals already in the work force or to those preparing for it.

For example, mentoring activities for adults and children seem to be gaining in popularity and may be an effective recruitment tool. An existing cooperative venture pairs members of the Women's National Book Association, an organization of people in many book and publishing-related fields, with Girl Scouts to encourage them to explore community-based, book-related careers. Clearly, library services are one of the most crucial and most easily accessible of these fields. The Boy Scouts of America and other community groups have comparable programs that can be explored or initiated by library managers.

A second recruiting strategy defined by the Carnegie Task Force suggests "multiple entry points into the [youth services] field." The variety of tasks within a library can serve to create these multiple entry points. It may be possible, for example, to hire students as library pages or technicians and provide formal and informal training as an introduction to or in preparation for a professional youth services position.[6] In small or larger libraries, "homegrown" staff may well be among the most knowledgeable and dedicated.

Additionally, working with community agencies has been determined to be an effective recruiting source for minorities.[7] It is vital for libraries to seek, hire, and value staff who reflect the cultural, ethnic, and racial diversity of the community and the society. Not only does this bring the library into compliance with Equal Employment Opportunity laws, it encourages use of library facilities by children and youth of diverse backgrounds.

Once the recruiter has identified some possible candidates, how are these candidates convinced to explore youth services in libraries as a career? One starting point is to identify the factors that often attract individuals to serving youth in libraries and communicate the rewards.

Speaking personally, I discovered early on that librarians who serve children and youth face a diverse, demanding job that can often extend beyond regular hours of service. At the same time, work as a youth services librarian offers a career with the potential for creativity, variety, and independence. It has allowed me to be an authority, not an authoritarian, with young people; provided an opportunity to see children grow cognitively, emotionally, and socially; and encouraged interests in many areas as well as the chance to bring these interests to life for (and with) young people. This work continues to present the challenge of working with a wide range of children, youth, and adults.

It seems obvious that the first step in trying to persuade others about the personal and professional pleasures of library service to youth is a broad knowledge of the field. In other words, it is important for those in the profession to remain knowledgeable about it, not only to recruit, but to enhance job satisfaction (of self and others), which is crucial in retaining staff. What are recent developments in the field? How do these developments affect library service to youth? Are different trends having an impact on these services?

Certainly, involvement with professional associations, both in and out of the library field, reading journals, and talking with colleagues should be standard operating procedure in keeping current, but often seem to be put on the back burner by working professionals. It is far too easy to get so involved in daily activities that we stop thinking and rethinking about what, why, how, and with whom we are involved. The primary commitment of youth services librarians and managers must be to our client group and to the provision of high-quality service.

It is equally important for youth services managers to develop a vision of what this work could or will be and to be able to articulate that vision to others.

For example, my personal vision rests in the conviction that librarians who work with youth and the significant adults in their lives will greatly reduce the number of adults with serious reading problems within one generation. In more optimistic moments, I may argue that the number of nonreading adults will vanish within that time. Whether or not those who hear me agree on this point, articulating this conviction has given us an opportunity to envision and discuss the future.

In addition to philosophical underpinnings, the successful recruiter must have an understanding and a thorough knowledge of the skills, competencies, and attitudes of a successful youth services librarian as outlined in *Competencies for Librarians Serving Children in Public Libraries*. Potential candidates must have more than a knowledge of developmental needs of children and youth and how library materials will meet their educational and recreational needs and interests; a healthy respect and appreciation for young people as well as their reading interests is crucial.[8] Recruiters must see beyond the resume and assess attitude in potential employees.

With candidates on hand and ready knowledge, an interview provides an opportunity for an employer to become acquainted with a prospective employee. Conversely, the interview provides an opportunity for a candidate to gain a sense of a potential employer. It is a chance for each to learn if a mutually beneficial investment could be in the making.

The interviewer, however, is also a recruiter. In attempting to fill a position with a well-qualified person who is likely to be a match for the position, there is also an attempt to persuade that person of the desirability of working within a specific organization. A position description delineates the basic duties of the job; the interviewer or interview committee, however, conveys the organization's philosophy, environment, and attributes.

There is some indication that the employment interview is predictive of job performance. In addition, structured interviews appear to be more valid than unstructured interviews.[9]

A structured interview is defined as one in which the same questions are asked of all candidates, although follow-up questions, or probes, may be asked. An interview committee, or panel, consists of several people asking questions of the candidate. It is highly recommended that questions be based on the position description to determine if indeed the candidate is well suited for it. Additionally, this is a recommended practice to avoid potential noncompliance with Title VII of the 1964 Civil Rights Act (as amended by the Equal Employment Opportunity Act of 1972), Title IX of the Education Amendments of 1972, and the Americans with Disabilities Act of 1990 (Public Law 101-336). This legislation precludes interviewers from asking about age, race, religion, marital or parental status, nonspecified job related physical data, or for information not relevant to the position.

In 1989, Campion and Arvey reviewed court cases "concerning discrimination in employment interviews," and recommended several practices, "including development of job descriptions, careful selection and training of interviewers, the asking of job-related questions, and use of committees to conduct interviews and make hiring decisions."[10]

No career path is without pitfalls; however, effective communication, beginning with the interview, can help both employer and candidate decide whether or not to invest the time and energy in each other.

Youth Services into the Future: Retention

In addition to recruiting, retaining good youth services staff is another challenge to administrators. Creating a stimulating environment through interdepartmental training is one strategy that may aid in retaining "plateaued" employees. As Barbara Delon observes, "Just because there are no vertical moves possible does not mean that employees have to stop growing."[11]

Interdepartmental training, sometimes called cross-training, not only increases employee knowledge, it can stimulate interest in other positions and functions, and develop a respect for the interrelatedness of each library unit and its unique functions. Too often it seems that library staffs are introduced to other departments in a trial by fire; an emergency creates the need to cover another unit. To be well versed in the work of other library units and to know how they relate to youth services can increase job satisfaction or at least reduce frustration. This cross-training must go both ways; youth services staff should be trained in other departments as staffs of other departments are trained in youth services. Youth services managers can work with other library departments to make interdepartmental training a regular activity.

Other strategies for retaining employees by keeping their jobs challenging include creation of teams of librarians to develop reading lists, summer reading program activities, and materials replacement lists. In other areas, librarians can take turns leading book discussions or developing the content for a staff meeting. Employees can be shared between libraries within a given library system or within a region to enhance programming activities and idea sharing. Of course, in-library training programs should be ongoing as they relate to issues, concerns, or projects of mutual concern to library staff. Certainly these can focus specifically on youth services issues or on broader concerns as they affect library services as a whole.

Library managers should also consider funding for support of formal education opportunities as a tool to retain good staff. Attendance at outside workshops and institutes stimulates staff and enhances networking and resource sharing. These activities continue to challenge plateaued employees and let them know that "no matter what their title or position in the hierarchy, they can make changes and grow where they are."[12]

Another way to retain staff is to encourage them to further their education with a degree in library science. As employers, libraries must maintain a dialogue with library schools that should be responsive to those organizations that will employ their students or hire their graduates. Research indicates that graduate programs in library science have strong regional appeal. That is, most library science students remain in their geographic area.[13] At the same time, there are fewer accredited programs from which to choose; nationally, the number of accredited library schools stands at fifty.[14] Perhaps a dialogue with library schools will lead to increased use of "telecourses" or distance education. Daniel Wood reports that "at a time when almost half the enrollment in higher education is part-time students, location and convenience are increasingly paramount," causing a "major structural change in the delivery of education . . . brought about by new TV technology."[15]

Managers can identify needs of potential or existing staff members and should encourage library schools to meet these needs through distance education course work, institutes, or short sessions offered at times conducive to broad employee participation. This facilitates continued involvement by experienced staff and provides support for those seeking professional advancement.

This support can take on other forms as well. Financial assistance may be available for graduate library school at the local, state, or federal level. The library can identify these funding sources (such as scholarships, grants-in-aid, and tuition reimbursement programs) and make information about them available to staff. Also, broad access to library resources through interdepartmental training or assignments as relevant to the employee's course of study enhances job satisfaction. Varied experiences allow the working student to combine the practical and theoretical, making each more meaningful.

Staff supported by the organization allows for promotion of youth services staff from within the ranks and helps to develop a youth services career ladder. The D.C. Public Library system has a "trainee" program for youth services librarians. The library provides in-library training, tuition support, and some administrative leave for employees enrolled in graduate library programs. After completion of a predetermined number of credit hours, the employee receives a noncompetitive raise. Once the degree is conferred, the employee (with supervisory approval) becomes a professional librarian. A recent reclassification in the D.C. Public Library system established a noncompetitive salary increase for professional librarians after one year of satisfactory performance. This has provided financial growth for longtime employees who do not seek supervisory duties. In addition, it allows some flexibility when recruiting new staff, since more experienced staff can be hired at the higher grade.

It may also be possible for larger library systems to increase job responsibilities and salary for youth services librarians as a means of retaining them. Too often it seems that in order to advance, youth services librarians must go into adult reference work. With a full understanding of the spectrum and impact of library service to youth, youth services managers can advocate for the development of these career ladders within the organization. This is not a new concept. In 1948, the Committee on Postwar Planning of the American Library Association suggested that "professional advancement as a subject or functional specialist must . . . be kept open. . . . The expert in bibliography or cataloging, . . . the children's librarian—these and other specialists should be enabled to advance in rank and salary without assuming important administrative responsibilities. . . . [This] will bring many librarians to satisfying positions which will permit the best use of their special qualifications."[16]

It is easier to retain staff when they are fairly compensated for work performed. Recent data suggest that gains have been made. The *ALA Survey of Librarian Salaries 1992* surveyed more than 1,200 libraries to determine average salaries paid to staff with master's degrees from accredited library education programs.[17]

Librarians' salaries increased an average of 3.6 percent between January 1991 and January 1992 with the exception of the children's or young adult services librarian. The survey indicated that salaries for these positions increased by 11.3 percent. Authors of the survey suggest that "there are several possible explanations for the unusual salary increase for 'Children's and/or Young Adult Services Librarian.' Shortages of people in the specialty have been noted for several years and low salaries are often cited as a reason. Indeed, this position has been at the lowest rank in all previous versions of this table."[18]

Though strides have been made, salaries should still be a source of concern and exploration at the local and regional levels. Youth services managers with other library administrators may seek pay equity studies or undertake reclassification projects to continue a serious examination of librarians' salaries. Salaries for youth services librarians must be brought into line with all other professional salaries and made competitive within a given geographic area.

Another strategy in retaining quality youth services librarians is to recognize and support the specialty. Many of those who go into library service for youth do so because of their commitment to the client group. At the same time, it appears that some public libraries are moving toward the "generalist" librarian. Many school libraries have vacant positions, are staffed with volunteers or aides, or have one professional librarian for the entire school district, rather than one librarian per building. It is vital to retain trained age-level specialists.

In fact, all librarians are age-level specialists. Adult services librarians readily acknowledge that the needs of a college student differ significantly from those of a homebound senior or of an adult learning to read. It must also be recognized that the needs of a toddler differ from those of a middle school student or the parent of a child in the primary grades—all of whom are served by youth services librarians. Carleton Joeckel noted in 1949 that "the complexities of our social structure, as well as of recorded knowledge, are making increased demands for specialization."[19] This is still true. Instead of moving to generalized or inadequate library service, libraries must encourage candidates to work with children and youth and provide necessary training for them. In doing so, library services are strengthened.

Equally important in retaining good youth services staff is maintaining administrative support and representation for youth services through the creation or retention of a youth services coordinator who is part of the administrative team. A position designated for this purpose encourages cohesiveness and understanding within the library and provides a spokesperson to articulate the positive impact of library service to youth both to other community groups and within the organization. Additionally, administrative representation for youth services creates a supportive environment in which resources and information necessary for effective, collaborative work are readily available. A healthy organizational environment in which effective communication, support, and cooperation are common is more likely to retain staff.

Individual libraries are not alone in their efforts to find and keep quality youth services staff. Recruitment and retention remain a national focus in professional organizations. The 1990s have been designated by the ALA Council as the "Decade of the Librarian." The council created a "recruitment assembly" comprising representatives from ALA units interested in the topic. In addition to working to create partnerships for scholarships and recruitment, this initiative supports a "broad based 'Each One Reach One' campaign to emphasize the importance of each librarian . . . helping to recruit new people into the profession."[20]

Each One Reach One: Recruiting for the Profession Action Handbook[21] is a useful document outlining general strategies and resources. The youth services divisions of ALA created an effective brochure to focus on the diversity of both the work and the staff. *Whatever You Like to Do . . . A Youth Services Librarian Probably Is Already Doing It* profiles professionals whose work reflects the diversity of the field and can be used with many ages (from high school to graduate school) to encourage further exploration of the field.[22]

In conjunction with the Decade of the Librarian, ALA's Standing Committee on Library Education (SCOLE) has recommended to the council a special project to examine crucial topics such as the skills, knowledge, and education needed by the future work force in libraries; the incentives needed to attract them; appropriate kinds and levels of education and how to best provide it; and the niche of the library in an information world.[23]

The youth services divisions of ALA also help to retain staff as they work to enhance communication and networking within the field and with related organizations. Consider, for example, the charge and the work of the Liaison with National Organizations Serving the Child and the Liaison with Mass Media committees of the Association for Library Service to Children, only two examples of organized collaborations within ALA and its divisions. The journals of ALA's divisions help to disseminate current research, program information, and information about topical issues to its memberships. Rather than working in isolation, youth services librarians are reminded they are indeed part of a far-reaching network.

Conclusion

Recruitment and retention begin with individuals invested in the belief that access to library service by youth can best be provided by knowledgeable, trained, and dedicated staff. All youth services managers help to recruit and retain staff as they continue to invest in the future through the services and staff provided today.

Notes

1. Public Library Association, *Statistical Report '92: Public Library Data Service* (Chicago: American Library Association, 1992), 46.

2. Judy Quinn and Michael Rogers, "122 Million Library Users Ask for More Technology," *Library Journal* 116 (April 15, 1991):14–15. This 1990 survey indicates that six out of ten people used a library in the previous year. See also two surveys contracted by the National Center for Educational Statistics (Washington, D.C.: U.S. Department of Education, Office of Education Research and Improvement) *Services and Resources for Children in Public Libraries 1988–89* (1990) and *Services and Resources for Young Adults in Public Libraries* (1988). Data from these surveys indicate that more than half of library users are children and youths.

3. American Library Association, 1990–1991 Council Document no. 58, "ALA Special Committee on Library School Closings Report." The status of 1992 graduates was reported by Fay Zipkowitz in "Fewer Graduates But Salaries Climb," *Library Journal* 118 (October 15, 1993):30–36.

4. Barbara Immroth, "Recruiting Children's Librarians" in *Librarians for the Millennium* by William Moen and Kathleen Heim (Chicago: American Library Association, 1988):37–46.

5. Carnegie Council on Adolescent Development, Task Force on Youth Development and Community programs, *A Matter of Time: Risk and Opportunity in the Nonschool Hours* (New York: Carnegie Corporation, December 1992), 84–88.

6. Carnegie Council, *A Matter of Time,* 88.

7. Mary G. Miner and John B. Miner, *Employee Selection within the Law* (Washington, D.C.: Bureau of National Affairs, 1979), 33.

8. For a complete discussion of competencies for youth services librarians in both school and public libraries, see: Association for Library Service to Children, *Competencies for Librarians Serving Children in Public Libraries* (Chicago: American Library Association, 1989); American Association of School Librarians and Association for Educational Communications and Technology, *Information Power: Guidelines for School Library Media Programs* (Chicago: American Library Association, 1988), 26–41; and Jane G. Connor, *Children's Library Services Handbook* (Phoenix, Ariz.: Oryx Press, 1990), 1–7.

9. Michael Harris, "Reconsidering the Employment Interview: A Review of Recent Literature and Suggestions for Future Research," *Personnel Psychology* 42 (1989):695.

10. J. E. Campion and R. D. Arvey, "Unfair Discrimination in the Employment Interview," in *The Employment Interview: Theory, Research and Practice* by R. W. Eder and G. W. Ferris (Beverly Hills: Sage, 1989), 61–73.

11. Barbara Delon, "Keeping Plateaued Performers Motivated," *Library Personnel News* 6, no. 4 (July-August 1992):7.

12. Ibid., 7.

13. William E. Moen and Kathleen Heim, "The Class of 1988: Librarians for the New Millennium," *American Libraries* 23 (November 1988):858–85.

14. American Library Association, 1990–1991 Council Document no. 58, "ALA Special Committee on Library School Closings Report."

15. Daniel B. Wood, "College Teleclasses Reach Remote Learners," *Christian Science Monitor,* March 23, 1990, 13.

16. Carleton B. Joeckel and Amy Winslow, *A National Plan for Public Library Service* (Chicago: American Library Association, 1948), 117.

17. Mary Jo Lynch, Margaret Myers, and Jeniece Guy, *ALA Survey of Librarian Salaries 1992* (Chicago: American Library Association, 1992), 22–23.

18. Ibid., 27–28.

19. Joeckel, *National Plan,* 114.

20. American Library Association, 1990–1991 Council Document no. 50, "The Decade of the Librarian: 1990-2000."

21. American Library Association/Office for Library Personnel Resources, *Each One Reach One: Recruiting for the Profession Action Handbook* (Chicago: American Library Association, 1989).

22. This 1989 brochure was a cooperative venture of the American Library Association, the American Association of School Librarians, the Association for Library Service to Children, the Young Adult Library Services Association, the Office for Library Personnel Resources, and American Library Association Communications.

23. American Library Association, 1991–1992 Council Document no. 14.1, "Library Education Plan."

Bibliography

American Association of School Librarians and Association for Educational Communications and Technology. *Information Power: Guidelines for School Library Media Programs.* Chicago: American Library Association, 1988.

American Library Association, Office for Library Personnel Resources. *Each One Reach One: Recruiting for the Profession.* Chicago: American Library Association, 1989.

Association for Library Service to Children. *Competencies for Librarians Serving Children.* Chicago: American Library Association, 1989.

Carnegie Council on Adolescent Development, Task Force on Youth Development and Community Programs. *A Matter of Time: Risk and Opportunity in the Nonschool Hours.* New York: Carnegie Corporation, 1992.

Connor, Jane Gardner. *Children's Library Services Handbook.* Phoenix, Ariz.: Oryx Press, 1990.

Moen, William and Kathleen Heim. *Librarians for the Millennium.* Chicago: American Library Association, 1988.

Osborne, David. *Reinventing Government.* Reading, Mass.: Addison-Wesley, 1992.

Peters, Thomas and Robert Waterman. *In Search of Excellence.* New York: Harper and Row, 1982.

Westin, Alan and Anne Finger. *Using the Public Library in the Computer Age.* Chicago: American Library Association, 1991.

Chapter 8

On Planning and Presenting New Staff Orientations

Kathleen Staerkel

What Is Orientation?

Orientation is a process that is designed to acquaint new employees with the library and its policies and to help them become productive members of the team as soon as possible. It is a planned effort that fosters and enhances the learning of job-related behavior. Through orientation new employees become familiar with the work setting, supervisors, co-workers, organizational values, expectations, corporate structure, and the formal employee-employer exchange relationship. Spending time with new staff members helps them develop feelings of belonging and acceptance, which avoids unnecessary anxiety, and they gain knowledge and skills that support their role and responsibilities in the library. In addition, during the process, supervisors determine the extent of new employees' proficiencies and experiences as they relate to specific job duties. This information is essential for planning the degree and depth of instruction needed for each new hire.

Orientation is the first phase of training that employees receive during their tenure with the library. Both training and development are used to motivate employees and encourage self-esteem and self-actualization. Training activities generally focus on structured, task-related skills. Development centers around less measurable aspects such as knowledge, decision making, interpersonal skills, self-awareness, attitude development, or motivation. Bittel describes the process of orientation as structured and systematic training based on "a careful study of what the job entails in terms of knowledge and skills and an orderly period of instruction provided by an individual (or individuals) who is well-versed in training techniques and aware of the possible pitfalls in the learning process."[1] Orientation is usually presented in two parts. The formal section, often conducted by administrative or personnel department staff, includes imparting information about what is expected of employees, employee benefits, the library's history, organizational structure, functions of each department, management philosophy regarding patrons and employees, and services offered. The job specific portion, conducted by the new employee's immediate supervisor, involves training and developing skills and knowledge needed to successfully carry out the job for which the employee was hired.

Successful orientations are customized to fit the needs of both the library and each new employee. According to Creth and Duda, an orientation program "encompasses a range of learning activities, including those designed to teach specific skills, techniques, and procedures, and those that provide employees with an understanding of organizational objectives as well as the general knowledge, concepts and attitudes necessary to ensure effective performance. Only a multi-focused program will achieve the desired quality of staff performance."[2]

Why Orient?

Libraries are complex organizations. Employees need to know the location of various departments and services, entrances and exits, staff facilities, and when appropriate, the location of other branches. "The quality of library service is dependent on the knowledge, skills, attitudes and resourcefulness of the staff."[3] Staff development, beginning with orientation, provides a framework to achieve a knowledgeable and competent staff.

When new employees begin a job, their enthusiasm and motivation are generally at a peak. Initial perceptions of co-workers, work environment, and culture will have a long-term impact. In addition, very few employees can immediately perform the tasks for which they were hired and must be instructed in the policies and procedures specific to the library. "Well planned, effective orientation programs create a bond that strengthens both organizational as well as departmental ties. New employees become part of the team quicker."[4] Additionally, spending time orienting new employees gives the supervisor an opportunity to learn their strong and weak points so that she or he can determine how best to deal with them on a day-to-day basis.

New employees need to believe they are noticed, appreciated, and depended upon. They have a strong need for information on their specific roles, on how those roles fit into the big picture, and on formal and informal organizational realities. Besides making new staff feel important, the time and attention given to orientation indicates to them the value placed on work and staff.

Training prepares employees to carry out their duties with greater efficiency and serves to give them confidence. In the absence of a training plan, employees learn haphazardly and often inaccurately. According to Creth, failure to orient can result in "higher costs to a library because of increased training time, the inability of employees to perform at acceptable levels or to maintain service standards, wasted work time due to errors, increased supervision, personnel problems, high turnover and low morale, and potentially a loss of credibility with the library's public."[5]

Orientation is one way of initiating and establishing good employee-employer communication and reducing the anxieties of a new environment and responsibilities. A thoughtful orientation that welcomes new employees can reduce turnover, thus saving the library valuable dollars. Reduced turnover and better trained staff mean better customer service.

Although training a new employee seems costly and time consuming, it is actually time efficient when compared with the hours it takes people to learn tasks on their own. According to Bittel, "The actual time for a new employee to reach job-competence standard is 16.3 hours for the unstructured way, compared with 4.6 hours for the systematic way."[6] Rooks notes that "effective training takes time, but good training will pay for itself in quality and quantity of work performed."[7] Since it is easier to learn fresh material correctly than to correct poor techniques and relearn job skills, a well-planned orientation saves money and time.

Who Should Orient?

Orientation is often a shared responsibility. Some larger libraries have personnel departments from which staff provide formal orientation programs. More often than not, the administrator or personnel officer introduces new staff to the library in a general orientation that includes a tour of the facilities, distribution of preemployment forms, benefit applications, and enrollment forms, and disseminates basic information on library policies and procedures, including pay and leave policies, parking situations, and working hours. The immediate supervisor takes over from there to train for department and job specifics.

Department managers usually orient permanent, full-time employees. Part-time employees, especially shelvers, are often oriented by the staff member who supervises their work. In these cases, the department head should meet and welcome new employees as soon as possible. Although instruction can be delegated, during the first crucial week it is probably best for the supervisor to act as the primary trainer. By doing this, all new employees receive comparable training. Also, supervisors get valuable first impressions concerning new employees' progress, how well they catch on, whether they are likely to succeed, and training deficiencies. It also helps establish a working relationship between the supervisor and new hires.

It is all right to delegate portions of the orientation to employees who are qualified to train and who have been given in advance job breakdowns with key points noted. If necessary, the department head should take steps to instruct everyone on the staff to whom the task of training is delegated. Sharing the responsibility frees the supervisor from spending so much time on the process. Also, it is sometimes easier for new employees to get acclimated to the job and library if they can relate to a peer. Additionally, when other members of the department assist, it helps build a commitment to a successful orientation and establishes a foundation for good working relationships among staff. Even so, a supervisor can never completely delegate training because she or he is ultimately responsible for the quality of work produced within the department.

Some of the qualifications needed by trainers include a thorough knowledge of jobs to be taught, the ability to relate to the worker's level of knowledge about the job, and an interest in aiding learners, which includes interacting and sharing with others and an outgoing and friendly manner. Trainers must be able to plan and prepare instruction before giving it, to express themselves clearly, and to affect and assess the performance of trainees. Finally they need to possess a positive and cooperative opinion of the work, department, library, supervisor, and co-workers in order to positively motivate new employees.

When Does Orientation Begin and How Long Does It Last?

Begin planning for a job-specific orientation during the interview process. Ask interviewees questions similar to "What aspect of this job would you like to learn first," "What are your expectations for the first day of work," "What projects are you most interested in learning about," or present a schedule of items you intend to cover during orientation and ask applicants which are most relevant.

The actual process of orientation can begin the minute an employee accepts the job. There is often a period of two or more weeks from the time a job is accepted to the actual starting date. This time can be used to disseminate preliminary information about the library, its structure, and purpose. Send copies of library publications. Key colleagues can call or write offering warm congratulatory messages and helpful hints on reading materials. There are several advantages to beginning orientation prior to the employee's starting date. Most of this phase of orientation is done on the employee's time. It gets new employees thinking about the library. Additionally, bits and pieces of information scattered over a longer period generally make a more lasting impression and ease the adjustment process so that new employees are more motivated and less apt to accept another job.

The length of each orientation depends on the importance the library places on orientation; resources available to schedule, coordinate, and conduct orientation; specific objectives of the orientation; and complexity of the job. A new page can be taught to sort and shelve books fairly quickly, while a new librarian can spend twelve to fifteen months learning different aspects of the job. Important as it is to orient permanent staff, it is equally or more essential for temporary staff. Their orientation needs to be done more quickly because temporary staff must become productive immediately. Temps do not have the time that permanent staff do, which is all the more reason for trainers to provide an organized program.

New employees at any level are flooded with information, and it is unusual for any two people to be able to absorb training material in exactly the same length of time. Trainers should review the amount and flow of information to be learned and determine how long a period to take to disseminate it. Brief sessions not to exceed two hours, spread over several days increase the likelihood that new employees will understand and retain presented information.

Before Orientation Begins

Three major phases of orientation include assessment, training and development, and evaluation. Assessment involves determining what needs to be taught, what techniques to use to disseminate this information, and how much time to set aside to complete the training. Using a form similar to that found in figure 1 will help supervisors identify training areas and completion dates. An effective orientation doesn't just happen without a plan. Once completed, everyone involved in the training process should receive a copy. But before beginning anything, it is important to gain support and commitment from administration. It is these managers who must identify needs, implement and coordinate library-wide activities, establish relevant policies and procedures, and ensure evaluation. In addition, they should provide guidance and assistance to other supervisors and trainers. Youth services managers can be involved by participating on a committee to develop a library-wide orientation program for general library information. Such a program insures consistent beginnings for all new staff members.

When developing both the general library and job-specific orientation programs, it is important for youth services managers to establish objectives. For assistance in developing objectives, secure ideas from the administrative managers, other supervisors, and the support staff who will be involved in orientation. Ask existing staff to identify the type of training that might be appropriate before beginning their particular jobs. Use interviews and questionnaires to obtain input from employees who participated in orientation programs and examine successful approaches used by other organizations. Of special interest may be information provided by the American Library Association (ALA) Association of College and Research Libraries (ACRL) Personnel Administrators and Staff Development Officers of Large Research Libraries Discussion Group, which maintains "an information exchange system to encourage and facilitate the sharing of information on each library's staff development activities, of training materials that have been designed for library training, and of evaluations of commercially produced programs, films, and other materials."[8] You may also request from the American Library Association's Staff Development Clearinghouse a list of sample staff development programs, policies, and manuals that they have on file and will send for use through interlibrary loan.

There are a number of benefits in establishing orientation objectives. Well-written objectives will improve training, help determine which teaching methods are appropriate, clarify what is expected of trainers and participants, and provide a basis for evaluating the program. Good training objectives include a statement of terminal behavior, a description of the conditions under which terminal behavior is expected to occur, and a statement that will be accepted as evidence that the learner has accomplished what was required. Objectives are more easily written when the information is laid out in a chart similar to that found in figure 2.

Add a time frame to this information to develop a job-specific goal such as: "Within one month after their starting date, new shelvers who are given a book truck and books will be able to sort and shelve one hundred books accurately every hour," or "By September 1 the new school services

---

Training Needs Identifier

Position: School Services Librarian

Employee _____   Department _____

Supervisor _____   Date _____

Instructions:

In column A, use the following numbers to rate the skill necessary for the employee to perform the job: 1 - very important; 2 - moderately important; 3 - not important.

In column B, place a check in the box if the employee already has the skill.

In column C, use the following ratings to indicate the need for training in each skill area: 1 - no need for training; 2 - moderate need for training; 3 - immediate need for training.

In column D, write the date by which each skill should be fully learned.

Skill	A Importance of skill	B Employee has skill	C Need for training	D Training completion
Plan age appropriate programs	_____	_____	_____	_____
Schedule school visits	_____	_____	_____	_____
Present programs	_____	_____	_____	_____
Evaluate programs	_____	_____	_____	_____
Call schools weekly for assignments	_____	_____	_____	_____
Use computer to locate library materials	_____	_____	_____	_____
Organize daily routine	_____	_____	_____	_____
Human relations skills	_____	_____	_____	_____

FIGURE 1. Sample Form for Identifying Training Needs. Reprinted with permission of Shoreham-Wading River (Shoreham, N.Y.) Public Library

Objective Development Chart

Terminal Behavior	Condition	Minimal Achievements
Shelve books	Given a book truck and books that need to be put away	Sort and shelve one hundred books accurately in one hour's time
Schedule 4th grade library skills programs	Given a school year calendar, a list of schools, their Learning Center Directors, and phone numbers, and the library meeting room calendar	Call all the learning center directors in September to set up days and times for their fourth grade students to visit the library for a library skills program

FIGURE 2.   Chart Used to Develop Objectives. Reprinted with permission of Longwood Public Library, Middle Island, N.Y.

librarian who is given a school year calendar; a list of schools, their learning center directors, and phone numbers; and a library meeting room calendar, will be able to schedule fourth grade library skills programs for the remainder of the school year." These measurable goals can be used later to evaluate performance.

In preparing for orientation, start with job descriptions. Review all the information each new employee needs and decide how much to distribute each day, week, or month throughout the orientation period. Consider what new employees need to be successful through the first week and structure the first session around this information. Some managers may find it useful to use a checklist similar to that found in figure 3 to organize pre-orientation planning.

Develop a list of knowledge and skills needed in the various jobs and then rank them. Break complex jobs down into simpler steps by observing each job, separating it into logical steps, and determining the key point for each step. The key point is the knack or know-how that makes the job go easier. Plan to teach the easiest steps first and then proceed to the most difficult. Be flexible in who does the training; decide who is best suited to orient new employees to specific information and train them to do it. When gathering materials, organize them in the order in which topics will be presented. In order to keep on track, managers may wish to write an agenda for the first day, such as that found in figure 4.

Be sure to set a time table for learning. One way to do this is to determine how important each skill is, record how much each worker already knows, and indicate what each worker needs to know. Then assess the amount of time necessary to train the worker on the new skills. Develop or acquire learning activities, training materials, and policies to support those needs. Set definite dates for completing training of each phase of the job.

Pre-orientation Planning

Check off each item as it is completed

_____ Prepare written orientation plan

_____ Designate work area and arrange for office supplies

_____ Collect and package required paperwork and forms for completion

_____ Free up own schedule to meet with the new employee

_____ Arrange for lunch the first day

_____ Discuss new staff roles with existing staff

_____ Train trainers

_____ Plan a welcoming get together

_____ Prepare first job assignment

_____ Collect copies of appropriate manuals and publications

_____ Other

FIGURE 3.   Pre-orientation Planning Checklist

Before the new employee's arrival, prepare his or her work space. Make sure it is clean and properly laid out with materials and supplies in their correct place. New employees should see the work place the way it is to be kept in the future.

In addition to preparing the workplace for new employees, managers must remember to prepare other staff before the new person's first day. New employees bring change. In some organizations, especially where there are a lot of long-term employees, there is a clannishness that may be actively hostile to new people. This hostility is usually caused by fear that the new person will in some way negatively affect the working environment. But the new person is also afraid of not fitting in or being accepted. The department head must allay these fears by reassuring existing staff and supporting new ones. One possible strategy is to assign current staff a small part of the training, or ask them to go to lunch with the new person.

Training Methods and Tools

When training, include a range of formal and informal activities. Use a variety of techniques that appeal to many senses since people learn differently. There are pros and cons to every method. When determining which ones to take, consider objectives, trainee involvement, complexity of the content to be presented, frequency with which the same information will be offered, skill level of the trainer, and costs. Remember that brief sessions scheduled over several days and intermingled with other activities help eliminate the problem of overloading new employees with too much information in a short period of time.

Personalized training is effective for skills enhancement but expensive and time-consuming. Training in groups is less expensive, but not often

Orientation Agenda

Monday, October 1 - Main library

Time	Activity	Presenter	Location
9:00 – 10	Welcome and introductions to key staff	John Jones Administrative Librarian	Business Office
10 – 10:15	Library history	John Jones	
10:15 – 10:30	Employee benefits	Mary Smith Benefits	Business Office
10:30 – 10:45	Break	John Jones	
10:45 – 11	Paperwork/Questions	Mary Smith	
11 – 12	Tour of the library	John Jones	
12 – 1	Lunch	Karen Lee immediate supervisor	Youth Services
1 – 2	Introductions to department staff	Karen Lee	
2 – 2:30	In-depth department tour	Assigned buddy	
2:30 – 3	Review job description	Karen Lee	
3 – 3:15	Break	Departmental staff	
3:15 – 4	Work space and simple first assignment	Karen Lee	
4 – 5	Review of assignment and wrap up/questions	Karen Lee	

FIGURE 4.   Sample First Day Orientation Agenda

practical in public libraries where one employee is usually hired at a time. One solution is to develop training materials in alternative formats, which then allows for improved quality in training, permits employees to use materials independently and at their own pace, and frees the supervisor from relying solely on time-consuming individualized instruction.

On-the-job training is a widely used method in which employees learn while trying to do the job. This is often done by *demonstration,* when the trainer shows trainees how to do a task and trainees then show how they have understood or mastered each task. This method is very personalized and requires a high degree of instructor skill. However, on-the-job training is probably the least expensive method of training, as it eliminates costs of off-site facilities, specialized teachers, and instructional equipment and materials. On-the-job training is also informal and easy to schedule. It is straightforward and individualized for each trainee. Another benefit is that employees do the actual work, not hypothetical or simulated tasks. The biggest obstacle in on-the-job training is making sure the trainer knows how to train and is willing to do so.

Classroom training can be used when several employees undergo training simultaneously. It provides consistency, presents fewer distractions, and allows instructors to be hand picked. Disadvantages of this method include limited participant interaction, expensive instructors, and lower retention than hands-on methods of instruction.

Lecture is a popular technique for providing basic facts on specific topics to many people. It is also used when much background information is required. Lectures are most effective when used with other training methods, as trainees can become easily bored by "talking heads." An additional problem is that the lecture technique provides for only one-way communication.

In *role play* the trainer establishes a drama that depicts a real-life situation. This assists trainees in anticipating situations and developing appropriate responses. However, not all employees are comfortable in role play situations, fearing that they will be made to look foolish. If role playing is part of the orientation, employees must be given adequate information beforehand so that they have some knowledge on which to base responses.

Case study is similar to role playing except trainees take presented material, analyze it, and propose a course of action. The same cautions apply.

Programmed instruction is self-instruction without the presence or participation of a trainer. Material to be learned is presented in text form or through a computer. Information is broken into small, logical steps, and trainees answer questions after receiving each small piece of information. Feedback is immediate and employees can review and repeat until desired learning is achieved. One of the strengths of this method is that it allows people to learn at their own pace. It also offers flexibility in scheduling. Programmed instruction can be low cost, portable, and very good, particularly for technical material. The method's biggest drawback is that it is often difficult to find and too costly to produce in-house.

Audiovisual presentations use sight and sound to assist trainers. Visuals speed up the learning process. According to Bittel, "Most of us use our eyes to pick up 80 percent of what we know."[9] Most presentations can be reused so that, in the long run, they save staff time and energy. Formats for audiovisual presentations include video, closed-circuit television, chalk board, films, slides, and flip charts. Audiovisual techniques work best when used in combination with other training methods.

Employment packets are a training tool that can ensure consistency. Prepared ahead of time, they can include standard forms and necessary explanatory literature, such as library organizational charts, maps of the facilities, policy and procedure manuals, lists of holidays and other important dates, information on fringe benefits, copies of performance appraisal forms, emergency and accident procedures, a sample copy of the library newsletter, etc. If different forms are needed for various levels of employees, prepare separate packets for each level. Instruct new employees to keep explanatory literature, particularly policies, since they are official documents that define their rights. Some libraries develop human resources manuals that contain synopses of detailed policies. The language in these manuals is less formal than that used in the policies, and the information is more concise. A human resources manual, sometimes called a staff handbook, can serve as a review or reminder of pertinent information, orients staff to the role of the library, and verifies and reinforces information in policy manuals.

An important orientation tool is a written orientation plan that helps staff keep on track. Part of this plan can be a checklist that helps both the trainer and trainees keep focused. It serves as a reminder of all the points that need to be covered during the orientation period. See figure 5 for a sample orientation checklist.

Components of Orientation

Planning is complete, candidates are selected, and now they are ready to start. Celebrate the arrival of each new employee by setting aside an hour and inviting existing staff to meet new hires. Supply refreshments. This puts new employees at the center of attention and provides them with an opportunity to meet co-workers in a relaxed, informal setting. If necessary, coach participants before hand to make newcomers feel welcome. When making introductions, exchange names and titles or job functions and tell something positive about the people being introduced. Identify resource people so new staff can find their way around the library.

After the get-together, move on to a more private session. Begin by answering the most basic questions new employees might have, such as "Who will I be working most closely with," "Where shall I park and which entrance into the building shall I use," or "Which aspect of my job needs to be learned first." Put new employees at ease by recognizing and acknowledging their anxieties and fears and work toward establishing a sense of belonging that acts as a solid base for team building. Be aware of the image you are presenting and make sure it is competent yet friendly. Remember that "good impressions are made within the first 30 seconds."[10]

Once you sense that your new employee is beginning to relax, move into the information session. Focus on the positives; negatives will be discovered soon enough. Distribute a packet of up-to-date and pertinent organizational information. Provide copies of their job description, job specifications, and job standards. Review the job description point by point. Show organizational charts and explain how employees fit into the structure. Go over the communication network and chain of command. Explain the library's current mission and roles and how the new employee's department contributes to both. Review working conditions, such as hours of work, meal times, coffee breaks, location of staff lounge and restrooms, pay day, dress code, and such. Offer plenty of opportunity for questions, but avoid telling too much too soon. The barrage of information presented to new employees can sometimes be overwhelming, so begin with essentials and fill in details later. Provide information verbally and then in writing (handbooks, policy manuals, etc.), and watch for nonverbal clues that indicate a feeling of being lost. The information and training that goes along with a new job is a lot to absorb, so repeat it several times and give information in small doses over a period of time.

Orientation Checklist

Indian Trails Public Library District
Young People's Services Department

Welcome to Indian Trails! Your supervisor, as well as the full-time and part-time staff members whom you work with, will fill you in on the following. As you complete an item, check it off. Plan to meet with your supervisor at least once a week during your first month of employment to go over these points, clear up any questions you encounter in your job, and be sure that you are working as expected. Within six months of employment plan to meet with your supervisor for an employee evaluation and to review this orientation procedure.

Administrative Services Orientation: to be completed on your first day of employment.

Tour of Library and introduction to staff

_____ Staff entrance
_____ Maintenance Department
_____ Outreach Department
_____ Library Cable Network
_____ Circulation Department
_____ Lobby area
_____ Administrative Department
_____ Library supplies
_____ Public entrance
_____ Board Room
_____ Public washrooms
_____ Staff lounge and kitchen
_____ Elevator
_____ Adult Services Department
_____ Technical Services Department
_____ Staff washrooms

Tour of Young People's Department and introduction to staff

_____ Work areas
_____ Public areas
    _____ New books
    _____ Magazines
    _____ AV kits
    _____ Cassette kits
    _____ Picture books, incl. cardboard, and paperbacks
    _____ Easy readers
    _____ Puzzles
    _____ Toys

FIGURE 5. Sample Orientation Checklist

_____ Records

_____ Compact discs

_____ Comic books

_____ Pamphlet file materials

_____ Fiction

_____ Young Adult Fiction

_____ Books on tape

_____ Paperbacks

_____ Parent Teacher Collection

_____ Foreign Language Collection

_____ Study prints

_____ Circulating reference

_____ Non-fiction

_____ Biographies

_____ Special assignment and holiday materials

_____ Cassettes

_____ Reference

_____ Video tapes

_____ Microcomputers

_____ CD-ROM's

_____ Bibliographies

Documents you will receive from the Young People's Department include

_____ Departmental function statement

_____ Departmental organizational chart

_____ Position job description

_____ Departmental staff meeting schedule

_____ Materials selection policy

_____ Page manual and list of duties

_____ Reference standards

_____ Patron Loan & Fine Policy

_____ Patron Behavior Policy

Documents you need to be aware of within the Department include

_____ Departmental procedures manual

_____ Information Notebook

_____ Emergency manual

_____ Time sheets

_____ Departmental notebook

_____ Reference tally/clip board

Continued

_____ Miscellaneous forms, such as

    _____ Americans with Disabilities Act

    _____ Application, employment

    _____ Authorized Work at Home

    _____ Cooperative Computer System

    _____ Incident

    _____ Interlibrary Loan

    _____ Leave of Absence

    _____ Overtime

    _____ Reconsideration Request

    _____ Sick Leave

    _____ Teacher's Advisory

You will need to become familiar with the following:

_____ Your own work area

_____ Operation of telephones

_____ Location of keys

_____ Operation of equipment (both staff and patron, circulating and noncirculating)

_____ Opening and closing the Department

_____ Meeting schedules (Board, Administrative Staff, and Departmental)

_____ Departmental supplies

_____ Performance review schedule and process

_____ Emergency procedures/safety procedures/fire extinguishers

_____ Kitchen clean-up

_____ Circulation procedures for AV equipment, periodicals, comic books, pamphlet file materials

_____ Placing reserves (in-house and interlibrary loan)

_____ Location of pay checks

_____ Hard to answer reference file

_____ Monthly reports (including location of past copies and giving input for current reports)

_____ Program information

_____ Trails Tales (Departmental Newsletter)

_____ Selection procedures/patron requests

_____ Teacher/homework procedures

_____ Book Bag Service

_____ Discipline problems

I have gone over this with the Young People's Department Head and feel that I understand its content.

EMPLOYEE _____ DATE _____

FIGURE 5.   Sample Orientation Checklist—*Continued*

Consider the following options for new employees on their first day:

Attend to social needs

Introduce to colleagues

Give tour of the facilities

Provide orientation packet and discuss important points in the packet

Outline organizational philosophy and objectives

Give brief history of the library

Complete necessary paperwork and give completion dates for other paperwork

Explain pertinent rules, regulations, procedures, and policies, including applicable city, state, and federal laws

Outline conditions of employment, such as working hours, punctuality, attendance, conduct, overtime, termination causes, and procedures

Explain pay periods; procedures; and benefits including salary, insurance, sick time, rest breaks, vacation, holidays, social activities, education benefits, pension, etc.

Take to lunch and reiterate welcome

Review job description, detailing job functions and responsibilities

Assign a task. New staff are eager to demonstrate their skills. An early assignment will challenge them, provide a sense of achievement and allow them to make a good first impression. Acknowledge what they did. Pay attention to the results and comment on them. This increases the likelihood that they will continue to work at the same high level in the future.

Before the day ends, spend positive, private time with them. Mention what was accomplished. Review progress made on any first work assignment.

Make a good parting impression

Within the first week, cover

Functions of other departments and how their department fits in

How performance will be evaluated

Acceptable and unacceptable behavior, including what is expected in terms of attitude, reliability, initiative, emotional maturity, personal appearance, etc.

Where to go for help within the library

Appropriate paperwork completion

More detail and training on specific jobs

Additional job assignments

Within the first month, cover

Opportunities for advancement

Opportunities for self-development

Formal feedback about orientation

Throughout the orientation process, remember to

Be sensitive to learner's moods

Be patient

Use open-ended questions

When training new employees, remember to start with simple assignments to build self-confidence and a positive attitude. Make these assignments useful and productive so employees gain a sense of accomplishment. Explain why assigned tasks are crucial to the success of the employee, department, and organization. Break complicated procedures down into smaller components. Teach one component at a time by demonstrating tasks, letting employees perform them under close supervision until they master them, then letting the employees proceed on their own. Correct errors privately and immediately through feedback to reinforce positive behavior and help employees move closer toward desired behavior. Once one part of a job is thoroughly understood, go on to the next.

As a trainer, try hard to be flexible. Remember that people learn better when actively involved in the learning experience and that each learner is different. Because of this trainers may need to adapt their plans throughout the training. Also, new employees learn quickly for awhile and then taper off to a temporary plateau. Take this time to reassure them that a halt in progress is normal and pile on the encouragement.

Avoid making the mistake of doing concentrated training during the employees' first week, and then forgetting about them. New employees need ongoing training for at least the first few months, and possibly much longer depending on the complexity of the job. Supervisors should hold regular meetings with new hires in order to monitor progress, provide support, and discuss any problems. Questions should be encouraged and treated with respect. Supervisors should also ask at frequent intervals if instructions are understood, and for new staff to explain in their own words a specific policy or procedure that was just covered. Department managers should hold regular meetings with trainers to assess progress of new employees and discuss how the orientation plan is working. Take nothing for granted. Remember also to put a copy of the orientation plan or checklist used in the employee's personnel file so that there is a record of training provided.

Evaluation and Follow-up

Management staff should evaluate the entire orientation program annually to be sure it continues to meet the needs of the library. Evaluation furnishes accurate, tangible information to assist further planning, improve decision making, and document achievements. It identifies program strengths and weaknesses, justifies the investment, and answers demands for accountability. It ensures that policies, planning, implementation, and funding are adequate and realistic.

In order to determine the success of an orientation program, build an evaluation into the plan at the design stage. Evaluation can consist of

> Participant reaction questionnaires handed out immediately right after the formal portion of the orientation and follow-up questionnaires some time later

> Assessment of knowledge gain, or what principles, facts, and techniques were learned

> Organizational consequences, such as tangible results in terms of reduced turn over, improved productivity, improved relations, etc.

Employees must practice constantly in order to become expert at a job, and important points must be repeated often. This makes follow-up extremely vital. Standard means for gathering follow-up and evaluative information are observation, questionnaires, and interviews. The sample questionnaire found in figure 6 uses both open-ended questions and ranking scales to gather data on the trainer, content, training methods, and materials.

When orientation is successful, new employees will feel part of the team right from the start. They will feel like they are making a significant contribution to the team and the library. They will have confidence in their supervisor and in the library, understand the rules and their reasons, not be afraid to ask questions, have a positive attitude, and feel good about coming to work and will be motivated to learn more. In short, a well-planned, thorough orientation will give new employees a good start to a rewarding and challenging job experience.

Orientation Evaluation

Name _____ Date _____

Position _____ Department _____

How well did the library meet your expectations for each item listed? 5 - exceeded your expectations; 4 - met your expectations; 3 - partially met your expectations; 2 - missed a lot; 1 - missed completely.

_____ I was made to feel welcome

_____ I was introduced to other members of the staff

_____ My co-workers were friendly and helpful

_____ My supervisor paid attention to me and made me feel welcome

_____ My orientation seemed well planned

_____ Library benefits were well explained the first day

_____ My work space was set up and waiting for me

_____ I received a tour of the library by a qualified person

_____ All the necessary paperwork and forms were available, and I received assistance in completing them properly

_____ I received a copy of relevant literature, such as the library's policy and procedures manuals

_____ I learned about the library's history and future plans

_____ My supervisor reviewed my formal job description with me

_____ I was invited to lunch the first day by my supervisor or a key individual

_____ I met people from other departments

_____ I was able to observe colleagues at work before starting a task

_____ I was given a specific job assignment along with instruction or training

_____ Office hours, dress code, sick leave, and other policies were explained

_____ I was shown the phone system

_____ I had opportunities to ask questions

_____ Payroll policies (and withholding) were covered my first day

_____ At the end of the first week I felt like a member of the team

Please answer the following. Use the back of this form if additional space is needed.

What, in your opinion, was the purpose of the orientation checklist?

Which section(s) of the checklist required additional time before they were covered adequately?

What, if anything, did you feel was omitted from the checklist?

What suggestions do you have for improving the orientation process?

FIGURE 6.　Sample Evaluation Form

Notes

1. Lester R. Bittel, *What Every Supervisor Should Know: The Basics of Supervisory Management* (New York: McGraw-Hill, 1985), 245.

2. Sheila Creth and Frederick Duda, eds., *Personnel Administration in Libraries*, 2d ed. (New York: Neal-Schuman, 1989), 118.

3. Ibid., 118.

4. Dave Day, "A New Look at Orientation," *Training and Development Journal* 42, no. 1 (January 1988):23.

5. Creth, *Personnel Administration*, 120.

6. Bittel, *Every Supervisor*, 248.

7. Dana C. Rooks, *Motivating Today's Library Staff: A Management Guide* (Phoenix, Ariz.: Oryx Press, 1988), 104.

8. Creth, *Personnel Administration*, 136.

9. Bittel, *What Every Supervisor Should Know*, 257.

10. Day, "A New Look," 20.

Bibliography

Arthur, Gwen, et al. *Library-Wide Staff Orientation and Public Services Training.* Philadelphia, Pa.: Temple University, 1988.

Bangs, David H., Jr. *Personnel Planning Guide,* 2d ed., revised and expanded. Dover, N.H.: Upstart Publishing, 1988.

Bittel, Lester R. *What Every Supervisor Should Know: The Basics of Supervisory Management.* New York: McGraw-Hill, 1985.

Branch, Katherine. "Orienting the New Library Employee." In *Practical Help for New Supervisors,* edited by Edward Garten and Joan Giesecke, 10–12. Chicago: American Library Association, 1990.

Brock, Susan and Sally R. Cabbell. *Writing a Human Resources Manual.* Los Altos, Calif.: CRISP Publications,1989.

Byars, Lloyd L. and Leslie W. Rue. *Human Resources Management,* 2d ed. Homewood, Ill.: Irwin, 1987.

Cadwell, Charles M. *New Employee Orientation.* Los Altos, Calif.: CRISP Publications, 1988.

Carrell, Michael R. and Frank E. Kuzmitz. *Personnel Human Resources Management,* 2d ed. Columbus, Ohio: Merrill, 1986.

Creth, Sheila and Frederick Duda, eds. *Personnel Administration in Libraries,* 2d ed. New York: Neal-Schuman, 1989.

Day, Dave. "A New Look at Orientation." *Training and Development Journal* 42, no. 1 (January 1988):18–23.

Fairfax County Public Library. *Page Package: A Training Manual.* Fairfax, Va.: Library Administration, 1987. Distributed by Public Library Association, a division of the American Library Association.

Fasick, Adele. *Managing Children's Services in the Public Library.* Englewood, Colo.: Libraries Unlimited, 1991.

Grensing, Lin. *A Small Business Guide to Employee Selection: Finding, Interviewing, and Hiring the Right People,* 2d ed. North Vancouver, B.C.: Self-Counsel Press, 1991.

Heyel, Carl and H. W. Nance, eds. *The Foreman/Supervisor's Handbook,* 5th ed. New York: Van Nostrand Reinhold, 1984.

Leibowitz, Zandy B., Nancy K. Schlossberg, and Jane E. Shore. "Stopping the Revolving Door." *Training and Development Journal* 45, no. 2 (February 1991):43–50.

O'Neill, Hugh E., ed. *Staff Analyst Associate Staff Analyst.* New York: Arco, 1983.

Phillips, Jack. *Recruiting, Training and Retaining New Employees: Managing the Transition from College to Work.* San Francisco: Jossey-Bass, 1987.

Ramsey, Ardella and Carl R. J. Sniffen. *A Company Policy and Personnel Workbook.* Grants Pass, Oreg.: Oasis Press, 1991.

Rooks, Dana C. *Motivating Today's Library Staff: A Management Guide.* Phoenix, Ariz.: Oryx Press, 1988.

Sager, Donald J. *Managing the Public Library.* White Plains, N.Y.: Knowledge Industry Publications, 1984.

Supervising and the Organization. New York: BFA Educational Media, 1981. VHS Videotape.

Tracy, Diane. *The First Book of Common-Sense Management: How to Overcome Managerial Madness by Finding the Simple Key to Success.* New York: William Morrow, 1989.

Truitt, Mark R. *The Supervisor's Handbook.* Shawnee Mission, Kans.: National Seminars Publications, 1991.

Chapter 9

Continuing Education

Mary Fellows

We live in a world of rapid technological change, and we claim a profession in which that change is even further exaggerated. It is no longer possible to train for a library career and be content that we have the skills and knowledge to successfully practice that career for the next thirty years. To avoid professional obsolescence, youth services librarians must make a commitment to learning that goes beyond the classroom and beyond the workplace.

Continuing education is ongoing learning that begins after formal education has ended. The orientation to a new job and the initial training period may both be considered "continuing education," but more generally associated with the term are the workshops, seminars, institutes, conferences, and in-service training opportunities attended by an employee once settled into a job.

A broad definition of continuing education describes it as a way of helping employees to grow and increase their confidence so that they can achieve more. According to Charles Kozoll, continuing education is "built on the assumption that all employees can continue to grow. If they are given an opportunity to learn a new skill or extend responsibility, they will accept it in a positive frame of mind, carry it out, and look forward to additional tasks."[1]

Importance of Continuing Education

This emphasis on the capability of employees to grow and increase their self-confidence is important in examining why continuing education is necessary. With many library schools closing, there is a decreased opportunity for would-be youth services librarians to obtain the M.L.S. Such a shortage of trained youth services librarians has forced more libraries to opt to hire staff trained in elementary education or other related areas. Given staff with no formal library training and no prospects of obtaining any, continuing education becomes absolutely crucial to the youth services manager in orienting these employees to the profession. As Terwilliger notes, "Patrons expect consistently excellent service from all employees; they make no distinction between job classifications and/or time on the job." Terwilliger also links the well-trained staff to positive public relations: in such a tight economy, she suggests, it reflects positively on the management to have "well-trained, knowledgeable personnel who demonstrate daily to taxpayers that their dollars are wisely invested."[2]

The rapid technological change in our society is a revolution magnified within the library profession. This is a significant change for all library staff, including youth services librarians. Delivery of library service electronically will become an ever more important part of our professional lives. Youth services librarians must make a commitment to continue learning in order to stay on top of current developments and use that knowledge to make the best choices for our patrons.

Another external factor in the importance of continuing education that goes hand-in-hand with rapid technological change is the increased competition in the delivery of information. Each day there are more sources of information available to users, and with the decrease in computer hardware prices, more consumers are able to access the information they need on their own, bypassing libraries entirely. There are also more independent information brokers willing and eager to play a provider role to users. While these independent information providers may be slower to target children than older consumers, they will do so eventually. If we have already become conversant with what they offer, youth services librarians will be in a position to be proactive to these changes rather than reactive.

In discussing continuing education as ongoing learning, it is important to acknowledge that while a formal library school education is exceptionally valuable, no course of study can practically cover every subject exhaustively in the time required to obtain a degree. Also, there is sometimes a significant gap between theory taught in academic institutions and actual practice, and once in the "real world," formal education usually needs to be supplemented and updated with additional training.

Benefits of Supporting Continuing Education

Youth services managers will accrue a number of benefits by supporting and encouraging continuing education among their employees. First, the library as a whole will develop. Organizations can only grow when the people in them grow. When youth services employees hone their skills, discover new abilities, and embrace new ideas, service to their clientele will improve, sometimes dramatically. Because of the high visibility of library service to children, this improved service will also enhance the library's reputation within the community, in turn creating new demands for services.

Second, continuing education keeps employees' jobs interesting and helps prevent burnout. There is a point in the careers of youth services librarians when "plateauing" occurs: there are no promotions available unless a decision is first made to leave a current employer or the youth services field. It is at this time that librarians are especially prone to burnout. Opportunities to learn new skills and be exposed to new ideas compensate for the fact that the employees have reached the top of their job classification level. Even among employees who are relatively new to the profession, a climate of openness to change will result in increased satisfaction with their work and increased productivity.

Third, exposure to new ideas and methods of service encourage risk taking and innovation among youth services staff. Often it is the example of someone who has tried a new program or service elsewhere that gives youth services librarians the courage to attempt it in our own library. Without exposure to these testimonials, many ideas remain just that.

Finally, continuing education is an opportunity to promote positive feelings about youth services librarianship as a profession and to promote a feeling of "team" by demonstrating to staff that their problems are universal. Continuing education occasions outside the library, especially, provide youth services staff the opportunity to get to know the professionals in their geographic area and to find a mentor. Conversations with other youth services librarians also help staff realize that there are certain problems that every youth services department encounters, and this realization gives them a chance either to learn strategies that might minimize their problems or feel good about the way they are currently handling a problem in their library.

Potential Problems

Despite the benefits of continuing education, there are some potential problems involved in helping staff develop. Employees may resist the idea of continuing their education. This may simply be an indication that the topic is not one particularly interesting to that staff member. But often the hesitancy goes deeper. Although it is hard to believe, there are some employees who feel they are doing their jobs perfectly and have no use for any information that may change their opinion.

There are also staff members who, whether for reasons relating to their complex personal lives or because of temperament, are content with a routine job. They simply want to do their work and go home, and are not interested in learning new skills that they will be expected to apply.

A lack of follow-through on the part of management can also dampen staff enthusiasm for obtaining continuing education. If there is no perceived organizational benefit for attending, such as compensatory time, payment of registration fees and travel expenses, or an invitation to share with a supervisor and other staff what was learned, staff may believe the experience not worth the personal expense and disruption of routine.

Some of these causes of disinterest, such as lack of management support, can be eliminated. But the more personal causes are harder to deal with. One solution is to write into each staff member's annual goals that she or he attend a certain number of outside continuing education experiences a year. With the full managerial support of the library, complete reimbursement for time and fees, and the knowledge that not attending will adversely affect their annual evaluation, most staff are able to overcome their disinterest.

Providing Continuing Education to Youth Services Staff

Outside Continuing Education Opportunities

Many libraries, particularly small ones, are best able to provide their youth services staff with continuing education by taking advantage of the workshops and conferences offered by professional associations and organizations. This is generally a useful and cost-effective strategy. State library associations and national associations such as the American Library Association (ALA) and the Public Library Association (PLA) offer frequent workshops, symposia, and conference programs on topics of interest to youth services librarians. Of particular note are the programs and regional conferences sponsored by the ALA divisions Association for Library Service to Children (ALSC) and Young Adult Library Services Association (YALSA). On the local level, regional library systems, state libraries, and library schools also have meetings and workshops built specifically around the needs of librarians serving youth. The best way to become aware of these opportunities is to be an active member of these professional associations.

While the continuing education opportunities offered by professional library organizations may meet most of your staff's continuing education needs, it is important to be aware that there are many other organizations that provide ongoing training which may be of interest to you as well. Other related professional organizations, such as Children's Reading Round Table (CRRT), the International Reading Association (IRA), or the National Association for the Preservation and Perpetuation of Storytelling (NAPPS) frequently offer useful workshops. Local universities and colleges often sponsor one-day training events and may also offer longer courses. Community-sponsored continuing education events, such as a speaker at a local business club, may fill a staff development need. An industry of instructors and consultants aimed at workers in a variety of types of organizations has sprung up in the last few years, and although often fairly expensive, these workshops may target the more general skills your staff needs to work on.

Sending youth services staff outside of the library for continuing education is a positive option in a number of ways. One is the avoidance of a large commitment of time on the part of the library in preparing an in-house workshop. Also, simply selecting a staff member to go to an outside workshop is in some cases a boost to the self-esteem of the employee. For some workers, concentrated development experiences may be the most effective learning strategy. Perhaps most importantly, outside continuing education experiences give staff members the opportunity to have contact with peers from other libraries who have the same kinds of problems.

There are drawbacks to outside continuing education experiences as well. Often these training sessions are fairly expensive in terms of registration fee, travel expenses, and time away from work. There is always the chance that the speaker will give the staff member a message with which you strongly disagree. Sometimes the publicity on an event does not accurately reflect the content, which may be too general or not applicable for the attendee. Also, at a workshop outside the library it is usually harder for the staff member to remember, bring home, and put into practice ideas from an intensive course. Lastly, if management does not also attend the workshop, it may prove difficult to provide the follow-up to the materials presented, which is an integral part of the process.

Internal Continuing Education Opportunities

A second option for providing staff with continuing education is for the youth services department or the library to do its own staff development in-house. This staff training may be a group effort, with the youth services manager or another professional assembling a workshop on a pertinent topic for presentation to the members of the department or the entire library staff.

Group efforts also encompass such things as field trips to other libraries or staff meetings. While a field trip to another library may put you in mind of a third grade trip to the donut factory, such "scouting expeditions" can be very fruitful, particularly if faced with a building project and the design of a new department. Although meetings with youth services staff may already be a regular part of the schedule, do not overlook the opportunity such meetings present for in-service training. But be aware that such training sessions cannot just be thrown together at the last minute. If monthly staff meetings are the norm, plan in-services semi-monthly or even quarterly in order to have time to prepare adequately.

A particularly effective group effort is to sponsor a regular youth services meeting with other librarians from the area, a training option for which travel expenses are usually minimal and registration fees nil. In addition to its cost effectiveness, this method will give staff members the outside support system they need and the opportunity for innovative, cooperative projects as well.

Self-developed continuing education is another option for managers who wish to help an employee grow. These efforts may take the form of a staff member and supervisor setting a development goal for the employee to accomplish, such as increasing knowledge of young adult literature by reading two young adult titles per month. Self-developed continuing education may also be as simple as a new assignment. Smart youth services managers have a ready list of tasks to be done if their staff appears bored.

There are some distinct advantages to in-house continuing education, particularly the group type. Generally, in-house workshops are most cost-effective in the long run. Management can control the information presented, and all staff can be given the same information at the same time. In-house continuing education can be an ongoing commitment, a series of training sessions on a regular basis, which often increases learning. Assisting the learning process is the close proximity of peers who are also being instructed, and with whom staff can exchange ideas. Perhaps most importantly, in-house training can be a valuable tool for youth services managers, allowing them to address problems, teach others new procedures, and analyze ethical issues as they perceive a need for information on these topics in their staffs.

The main disadvantage of home-grown programs is the time involved in planning and implementation, as well as the possibility that if staff are familiar with the speaker, that familiarity may make them tune him or her out. The old adage about the expert being someone from fifty miles away often holds true here; however, there are strategies to ensure the success of in-house continuing education.

Making In-House Continuing Education Effective

Create a Climate Conducive to Learning

Developing a successful in-house continuing education program requires preliminary attention to creating a climate conducive to learning. In such an atmosphere, staff members are encouraged to pinpoint weaknesses and inadequacies. Rather than management viewing these admissions as cause for punishment, they are instead considered an indication of interest in progress both for the organization and for the person.[3] It is this action on the part of employees that will aid managers in making sure continuing education topics are relevant to the needs of the staff.

Another factor in creating a climate conducive to learning requires managers to make it clear to staff that they do not consider their employees to be substandard, but good employees who may be able to benefit from the experience. Also, when structuring continuing education experiences it's important to make sure the employees are not being taught as children, but as respected adults who have important life experiences. As Davis and McCallon suggest, the wise trainer does not ignore life experience, running the risk of insulting adult employees, but instead builds on it or even taps into it as a contribution to the continuing education experience.[4] It is also important to remember that individuals learn differently, and to build variety into a program and be flexible enough to adapt it if audience reaction warrants a change in approach.

Another method of increasing adult learning is to acknowledge staff members' pride by building self-direction into the learning experiences.[5] For example, by allowing staff input into the best method to train on a particular topic, youth services managers demonstrate respect for their employees' abilities and self-knowledge. This involvement prevents the knee-jerk reaction that some employees may have to authority or training "handed down from on high." Davis and McCallon point out that training derived simply from authority may be resisted and will elicit the learned responses adults have to authority: buck it, bow to it, endure it, or welcome its helpfulness.[6] By including employees in presenting the training, the more negative responses can be tempered, if not eliminated entirely.

When planning any continuing education experience, it's likewise necessary to remember that adults have "real decisions to make and real problems to solve,"[7] and training should not waste their time. If an idea or change in procedure can be communicated equally effectively in a memo, do not take up the group's time by going over it together.

The leader's role in creating a climate conducive to a positive training experience is key. Management must lead by example, taking an active interest in developing their own skills and careers. Managers must also be available to help employees, assisting them with patience and empathy rather than impossibly high expectations. It is frightening and very difficult for some employees to learn new things, and supervisors must encourage questions, even "smoking them out" if necessary. Sincere compliments at progress and regular evaluation also aid the learning process.[8]

Assess Department or Organization's Needs

Before planning a continuing education experience for your staff, it is necessary to determine what the training needs are. It is important to involve staff in this process because involvement in the process will give them ownership of the outcome, which is then more likely to be positive. With staff, assess the department's continuing education needs by identifying problems or reviewing professional standards such as the *Competencies for Librarians Serving Children in Public Libraries* and using them as a document to uncover weaknesses.

Frequently, the youth services manager will have ideas about the areas in which staff needs to become stronger, but leading employees to that realization and then planning staff training with their help and cooperation will enable management to provide a better learning experience. In assessing needs, training should be thought of as an ongoing and related series of activities rather than quick "problem solves." An hour-long training session may indeed solve a staff problem neatly, but it will be much more effective within a framework of continuing commitment to growth.

Choose a Format

There are numerous techniques through which to disseminate information. These may be divided into two groupings: presentation techniques and application techniques.

Presentation techniques are mainly used to provide new information and include such methods as panel discussions, speaker and reactor panels, debates, videos, teleconferences, demonstrations, exhibits, and the most common—lectures. Panel discussions are used most effectively to present varying viewpoints on or experiences with a particular topic and should be followed with a question and answer period. Speaker and reactor panels are useful in presenting controversial or startlingly new information in areas in which the participants are inexperienced. Debates are most effective in providing sharply different viewpoints on a familiar issue.[9]

The best use of videos is to provide the perspective and persuasion of a nationally known expert or to show viewers a new product, service, or skill that would otherwise be unavailable to them. Demonstrations are the ideal way to teach new manually based skills or to introduce new technology or equipment. Exhibits can also provide the staff with some familiarity with new technology before actual training, which can be a time saver. Lectures by a single speaker are most effective in presenting expert information on a noncontroversial topic.[10] Teleconferencing is another way to provide continuing education opportunities.

Application techniques, by contrast, give participants a way of applying the new information to real-life situations. These methods include case studies, role playing, games, and discussion groups. Case studies are a way to have participants apply new conceptual skills to an environment that has similarities to the one in which they work, without activating their preconceived ideas about their own organization. Discussion groups, on the other hand, provide a method to discuss one's own situation and receive others' reactions to it, as well as hearing stories about other environments. Role playing can allow staff members to practice a new or difficult skill in a safe environment, while games can teach and reinforce a concept or skill in an entertaining way. Be warned, however, that not all people are comfortable playing games in a work environment, particularly games in which they fear they will be made to look foolish. Choose games wisely, and explain them thoroughly for the most positive results.

The best learning experience is likely to combine both presentation and application techniques. Depending on the complexity of the topic, coordinators may want to choose one presentation technique and several application techniques, or vice versa. There are only two rules: avert audience boredom by injecting variety, and choose the techniques that will be most effective for the information to be covered. Program effectiveness increases as participants are interested and involved.

Whatever format or formats are chosen, it is always beneficial to provide handouts. This does not mean that the main part of the presentation should be reproduced for the participants and read to them. Such a technique is unfailingly insulting, particularly to librarians. The key is to extract meaningful information and reproduce it in such a way that participants may use it to later refresh their memories on the salient points of the learning experience. Many speakers prefer to give their audience an outline of the material to be covered, and this can be a very useful handout; however, a few cautions: the outline must be relevant to the speaker's program, and not the extra information that she or he hopes to have time to cover. It should also be brief and complete but not overly detailed.

Choose Presenters

In choosing presenters, youth services managers have a choice between selecting an outside paid speaker (if the budget and management allow) or using internal or local experts who will do the program for little or no fee. Using an instructor outside the organization can be an effective way to handle a sensitive topic. Even though most staff will understand that the viewpoint presented is management's viewpoint, it is not management doing the actual persuading, and therefore it may go down a little easier.

Also, the staff may simply hear an outside speaker better, if the habit to tune out management is strong.

With purchased programs or presenters, it is imperative that youth services managers do their homework first to be absolutely certain that the training package or consultant is what is needed at this time. Also, even though it may be self-evident that the staff needs a good talk about censorship to bolster their flagging ideals, and a person reputed to be eloquent on the subject is available locally, make sure his or her message is the one you want to impart to your staff. Talk to colleagues who have used this person or at least heard the speaker, and weigh their opinions. It is very risky to bring in a speaker about whom little is known, even one who has a position as a professional consultant. Anyone can call herself a consultant; the title is no guarantee of competence.

The other option for youth services managers is to engage colleagues within the system or local associations who will do the presentation without remuneration. But even if the speaker is not being paid, she or he should still be checked out. The staff will not know or care if the library management pays an instructor to present a topic to them, but they will know if the speaker does a lousy job. Free presenters should be researched just as carefully as paid ones.

It is almost always a good idea to use peers of the audience whenever possible. If finances preclude hiring an outside presenter or the youth services manager has the expertise to train on a particular topic, involve a staff member to work jointly on the session. Consider particularly involving the staff member who is weakest in that area, as the best way to really learn something is to have to teach it to others. Having a staff member present a topic bolsters not only the self-confidence of that employee, but can also increase the satisfaction of the entire staff. The fact that the boss asks a staff member of equal knowledge to help with a training on a particular topic shows other employees that the staff's abilities are being acknowledged. To retain the audience's interest, youth services managers should vary the presenters on complex topics as much as possible. This also involves more staff in the training.

Strategies for Successful Workshops

There are a number of steps youth services managers can take to ensure a successful continuing education experience for their staff. First, it is important to set clear objectives for the training. The youth services manager must know what is to be accomplished and have a clear understanding of how best to accomplish it. Doing this will enable a more effective evaluation of the program when it is finished, and overall create a more valuable experience.

Second, youth services managers should be careful to choose an appropriate amount of information for the time available, and vice versa. Do not, for example, try to cram a workshop on reference service into half an hour. Likewise, if an outside speaker is being brought in to cover a particular topic, the program coordinator should talk with the speaker in advance so that arrangements can be made for a training session long enough for him or her to adequately cover the subject. Trying to crowd too much information into one session will result in a poor learning experience and frustrated employees who will not be willing to tackle the subject again soon.

It is also important for those who are structuring the continuing education experience to organize the information logically and break it down into small segments. Doing so allows participants to organize the information in their own minds. Strive for clarity in the way in which the information is presented and encourage the presenters to rehearse; the more smoothly the training goes, the better the learning experience will "take."

When introducing a continuing education session, begin by putting it into the context of other training sessions or current training goals. Once finished with the bridge building to past continuing education efforts, the presenter can easily move into the theories underlying the current session.

Using teaching techniques that acknowledge participants as adults and individual learners is crucial. As discussed earlier, adults have life experiences that they can relate to the training, so it is essential to encourage questions, even "smoke them out" if necessary. Also, presenters should allow participants to discuss the particular way they will put a technique or process into practice. While it is necessary to keep to a training schedule, presenters should try to avoid cutting off discussion that can lead to clarifying questions. If the continuing education is procedure related, such as training on a new procedure for reserves, employees should be allowed to try the new practice immediately and be given immediate feedback.

Post-Training Responsibilities

After the workshop, youth services managers must provide constant support for employees working on their new skills, and regular reinforcement of the skills learned. This could take the form of a few minutes' conversation at a monthly staff meeting about how the learned techniques are working. It is also important to make compliments and evaluation a regular part of the job, remembering to praise in public and correct in private. In order to reward those staff members who are enthusiastic and diligent about learning new skills, combine recognition with assignment of new work periodically. Care should be taken that the employee is not already overloaded, and that the new work is not a drudge job, but an interesting or challenging project. Also, successful continuing education on the part of the employee should be tied if possible to upward mobility: either a new job, a new job title, or a raise.

Last, youth services managers should evaluate the continuing education experience offered and follow up on it with the employee. Evaluation may be done either formatively (while the workshop is taking place) or summatively, after it is over. Formative evaluation can be accomplished by observing such things as the puzzled looks on employees' faces or the type and number of questions asked during the training. Summative evaluation may include review of the evaluation forms you asked participants to fill out, and by judging how well the continuing education met the stated objectives.[11] Both will be helpful in assisting the youth services manager in structuring an even more effective continuing education experience in the future.

Managers should make it a practice to follow up on continuing education experiences with the employee, either through informal discussions or in a forum such as monthly meetings. It is also useful to check with the employee a number of months after the training to see how the instruction was put to use.

Conclusion

Continuing education for youth services staff, whether done in-house or accomplished through outside sources, is an investment of time and money that may seem to youth services managers an impossibility given current staffing and workload. But staff time in this case is like the old adage about money: you have to spend it to make it. Staff time spent in continuing education activities will lead to employees who are more enthusiastic, more content, more flexible, and more productive in their jobs. In turn, this confident and positive outlook will be communicated to the patrons, and the end result will be what we all are striving for: excellent library service to children.

Notes

1. Charles E. Kozoll, *Staff Development in Organizations* (Reading, Mass.: Addison-Wesley, 1976), 35.
2. Gail Terwilliger, "Training for Children's Services," *North Carolina Libraries* 48 (Winter 1990):246.
3. Kozoll, *Staff Development,* 72.
4. Larry Nolan Davis and Earl McCallon, *Planning, Conducting, Evaluating Workshops: A Manager's Guide to Staff Development* (Austin, Tex.: Learning Concepts, 1975), 4.
5. Kozoll, *Staff Development,* 84.
6. Davis, *Planning,* 5.
7. Ibid.
8. Kozoll, *Staff Development,* 27.
9. Public Library Association, "Program Format Ideas," Attachment 2.
10. Ibid.
11. Joe Washtien, *A Guide for Planning and Teaching Continuing Education Courses* (Washington, D.C.: The Continuing Library Education Network and Exchange, 1975), 38–39.

Bibliography

Association for Library Service to Children. *Competencies for Librarians Serving Children in Public Libraries.* Chicago: American Library Association, 1989.

Davis, Larry Nolan and Earl McCallon. *A Manager's Guide to Staff Development.* Austin, Tex.: Learning Concepts, 1975.

Kozoll, Charles E. *Staff Development in Organizations.* Reading, Mass.: Addison-Wesley, 1974.

Ryan, R. Lloyd. *The Complete Inservice Staff Development Program.* Englewood Cliffs, N.J.: Prentice Hall, 1987.

Terwilliger, Gail. "Training for Children's Services." *North Carolina Libraries* 48, no. 4 (Winter 1990):246–52.

Washtien, Joe. *A Guide for Planning and Teaching Continuing Education Courses.* Washington, D.C.: The Continuing Library Education Network and Exchange (CLENE), 1975.

Chapter 10

Staff Evaluation

Marie C. Orlando

If speaking in public is a person's most dreaded activity, then evaluating one's fellow employees is probably not far behind. How do you commit to official written form your honest observations about the way a colleague is performing? How do you talk to another person about the quality of her or his job performance? Yet management books tell us this is necessary, our libraries and parent organizations have set up a procedure for this, and deep down we know it should and must be done in order to run our departments properly and productively.

In the usually benign atmosphere of the youth services department, the staff evaluation process may be even more difficult than in other departments in the library. The egalitarian relationship between supervisor and staff is probably more apparent here. Unless the library is very large, the youth services supervisor is likely to perform other than supervisory functions, frequently moving back and forth between the supervisor and colleague roles. So when evaluation time rolls around, a supervisor is required to step back, study, and make a value judgment about how well each staff member is performing, and then relay that information to a higher authority and to the employee. This can be uncomfortable indeed!

But the reality is that in most libraries, as in most other public and private sector organizations, annual staff evaluations come with the territory of supervision and require skills and techniques that often do not. The library may have a procedure and form to follow, but seldom is there any kind of training to help a supervisor deal with this formidable challenge. And yet there are many tools available and much practical advice that can be brought to bear at evaluation time.

An important thing to keep in mind is that evaluation time is continuous. Although formal evaluations may take place on a particular schedule, staff performance is probably being evaluated informally almost every day. Every time a staff member is complimented on a job well done, every time a suggestion is made as to how something might be done more efficiently, every time the members of a department sit down to brainstorm how a particular procedure needs to be revised to improve service to the public, evaluation is taking place. Consequently, at formal evaluation time there should be no surprises, and written evaluations will probably be no more than a printed reiteration of what has already been communicated verbally. In a well-functioning library, evaluation is constantly taking place as staff members strive to provide the best library service possible.

Most management guides will tell you that formal evaluation should be done once a year. Sometimes it is the same time of year for everyone and sometimes it coincides with the employee's anniversary. In many instances it is related to approval of a salary increase, either merit or step. The first step, of course, is to know your library's policy and to be prepared to submit your written evaluations on time. But the real key to making your staff evaluations easier to do and more effective in the long run is to set up a procedure of ongoing evaluation. Before considering the nuts and bolts of the formal evaluation process, we will explore the philosophy and techniques for ongoing evaluation.

Ongoing Evaluation as Part of the Planning Process: Goals and Objectives

Probably the easiest way to overcome the discomfort of evaluating colleagues is to approach the process from a perspective of what is good for the department and the library. If you work with a plan including a schedule of goals and objectives to be completed, then it becomes almost formulaic to determine whether each member of your department "team" is contributing to their achievement. While the language and structure of a statement of department goals and objectives is not the subject of this chapter, it is important to note, particularly as it has a significant impact on the staff evaluation process, that goals and the means devised to reach them should be clear, concrete, measurable, and time-limited. (A thorough familiarity with *Planning and Role Setting for Public Libraries*[1] and *Output Measures for Public Library Service to Children*[2] will be extremely helpful when attempting to articulate your goals and objectives and the means to measure them.) For example, if you have decided that a goal for your youth services department is to improve reference service over the next six months, it will be easier to measure your success and the performance of your staff in achieving that success if one of the objectives toward that goal includes an increase of 25 percent in the fill rate on reference questions. Tracking the pattern of fill rate and correlating it with staffing schedules will demonstrate how individual staff members are doing in helping the department reach its goal. This kind of specificity ensures that when we evaluate performance we are actually evaluating performance and not attitude or personality. Sometimes it is valid and necessary to discuss attitude with a staff member and this is best done in an informal, face-to-face encounter. But this issue should be part of the formal performance evaluation only when a poor attitude or spirit of cooperation is affecting performance. This will be addressed again later.

Ongoing Evaluation: Job Description

We have all seen it—the ad for a youth services librarian calling for a dynamic, creative self-starter with people skills, the ability to work under pressure, meet deadlines, and make the most efficient use of the resources at hand. We would all like to think of ourselves as this person, and indeed, many of us have been. This is probably why we now find ourselves in the management role. From this perspective we would now like to think that the members of our staff fit this ideal description and perhaps some or all of them do. The problem is that when we are evaluating our staff, this description does not begin to help us determine whether a staff member is doing a satisfactory, unsatisfactory, or super job in performing on a day-to-day basis. What is needed here, then, is a job description for each position in the department that gives a clear, concise, and complete picture of exactly what is expected of the person who does that job. If your library does not have such job descriptions, here is a good way to develop them for the staff of your department.

Break down all the duties of the youth services librarian; be sure to list every one, including those that must be done on a daily, a weekly, a monthly, or a seasonal basis. They should include things such as

    providing readers' advisory

    answering reference questions

    responding to telephone reference questions

    preparing reports

    planning and conducting storyhour

    ordering materials

    planning programs

    preparing publicity

    visiting schools

Give a full yet concise description of each, e.g., "planning programs: collecting information on types and providers of programs; conferring with other staff in the department to determine type of programming based on departmental goals and scheduling; contacting performers; confirming the date, time, and fee in writing; arranging for meeting space; preparing an introduction; planning publicity; and working with other staff as designated to produce and distribute publicity." Again, being specific on the requirements of the job make it that much easier to measure the level of success in performing these duties. This procedure of formulating a clear job description can and should be done for staff at every level: librarian, clerical, and page.

Ongoing Evaluation: Competencies and Standards

Now you have the "what" of a job description. Next you need the "how" or, more to the point, "how well." For this, the Association for Library Service to Children, American Library Association has provided a wonderful tool: *Competencies for Librarians Serving Children in Public Libraries*.[3] It is highly recommended that every public library have a copy of this publication. It breaks down into seven broad categories the areas of expertise that need to be developed by youth services librarians, defining within each category the components of activity that support that competency. For example, Competency IV, Materials and Collection Development, involves: A. Knowledge of Materials, B. Ability to Select Appropriate Materials and Develop a Children's Collection, and C. Ability to Provide Patrons with Appropriate Materials and Information.[4] Then, within each of these subcategories, anywhere from three to nine specific activities describe how that competency is demonstrated. The *Competencies* are invaluable for several reasons that relate to our discussion. First, they present the performance standard for librarians to result in the ideal functioning of a youth services department. Second, they provide for setting staff development goals and a means to achieve them. Finally, they serve as a guide to developing a format for formal evaluation.

Ongoing evaluation is hard work, but it pays off in many ways. First, it identifies any problems that, if ignored, might lead to serious deterioration of library service. Good communication in an atmosphere of trust means that staff members understand their supervisor's vision for the department, are aware of their place in that vision, can comfortably agree or disagree with the means to achieve that vision, and can work through solutions to any problems that arise. It also means that a supervisor can articulate clearly what is expected and why, is open to staff input, and is flexible in deciding strategies to accomplish goals.

All that may sound very idealistic but there are some tools and techniques to help the process along. Developing an atmosphere of trust is an important place to start. If your staff is confident that you are being honest and open with them and that you will support them, even when they make mistakes, they will be much more open to taking direction, initiative, and even criticism. Staff meetings on a regular basis are an effective way to strengthen communication and assure that everyone is properly informed. While it is often difficult to make time in the department's busy schedule for staff meetings, their importance cannot be stressed enough. Make an effort to schedule them when the majority of staff members can attend, including part-timers. Have the proceedings committed to writing for those who could not be there.

Facing Problems

As important as ongoing evaluation is to keeping a department running smoothly, it is even more vital when problems arise. If evaluating one's colleagues is difficult, then conducting an interview with a staff member who is not performing well is even more so. The process will be eased if there is already an atmosphere of trust within the department and, while it will never be easy, a few guidelines will help it to be less painful. The monthly newsletter *Communication Briefings* included, in its January 1993 issue, this helpful advice:

When you must give corrective feedback, make it more effective by giving it some structure with this format:

Let the employee know you're concerned and why.

Cite an example of a good effort by the employee to show that the employee can do what is expected.

Give specific instances that concern you about the employee's behavior.

Heighten the employee's sense of responsibility by describing the effect of that behavior—and make the employee aware of the consequences.

Give the employee a clear picture of the standard that he or she must meet. Even if the standard has been set earlier, restate it.

Ask the employee to describe why he or she acted that way. But be sure to steer clear of a "Why haven't you?" type of challenge.

Ask the employee to suggest solutions. But be ready with your own solutions in case the employee doesn't offer any.

Decide together on a plan to correct the behavior.[5]

This procedure can be used when discussing employee attitude or performance problems between formal appraisals.

In addition, it is always helpful to keep a critical incident log. You may think you are going to remember all of the examples of problem performance but the reality is that you're not. Each time an occasion arises when a staff member has not performed as required, confront the employee quickly. Briefly jot down the incident including the date, the circumstances, and the response, and file it. When the time comes for your disciplinary interview, you will have concrete examples upon which to draw. Remember to do the same when a staff member has performed particularly well. It will give you a basis for a positive evaluation and will also smooth the way for any negative comments that need to be made.

Formal Performance Evaluation

There are probably as many different approaches to staff evaluation as there are staffs to evaluate, but there is one element each should have in common. Staff evaluation must always include an articulation of how close the staff member has come to the satisfactory performance of the specific duties to which she or he has been assigned.

The format of the formal, usually annual, evaluation can vary from the most casual "let's sit down and have a chat" method to a highly structured process involving a checklist, written report, rating formula, face-to-face interview, sign-off, and salary increase recommendation. Your library will probably require you to use a format already in place, but whatever the format, certain basic objectives apply to any formal evaluation. In her chapter on performance appraisal in *Practical Help for New Supervisors,* Joan Giesecke lists these objectives: "1) to provide a method for recording unbiased impressions of an employee's performance, 2) to allow for consistency in documenting performance among those making evaluations by using standard forms, and 3) to provide a method for planning goals and objectives for the next year."[6]

She goes on to give as an example this procedure for preparing an effective performance appraisal.

To complete a successful appraisal interview, a supervisor should carefully prepare for the interview by following these steps:

Study the position description. Know what the employee should be doing. Check goals and objectives.

Evaluate your performance as a supervisor. Have you helped or hindered the employee's performance?

Complete the written appraisal using knowledge of past performance, critical incidents, and observations. Do not overemphasize recent events. Consider the employee's performance for the whole year.

Prepare for the appraisal interview. What results do you expect from the interview?

What contributions has the employee made? Is the employee working up to his or her potential? Does the employee know what is expected? What strengths can you build on? What training or retraining is needed?

Schedule the interview. Find a quiet place where there will be no interruptions. Allow plenty of time to discuss performance, goals, and objectives.

Review the form with the employee. Listen carefully to the employee's comments. Ask open-ended questions. Keep the conversation job related. Discuss new goals and objectives.

Discuss areas for improvement. Develop concrete plans for these areas. Develop a schedule for reviewing objectives and progress in these areas. Be candid and specific in discussing behavior. Include the employee's comments on the form as needed.

Close the interview. Summarize major points and goals, objectives, and areas for improvement on which you have agreed. Plan any needed follow-up. End the interview on a positive note. The appraisal is an opportunity to plan for improved performance and to reward successful completion of existing goals and objectives.

Sign the appraisal form. After the discussion with the employee, the supervisor and the employee should complete the written appraisal form according to the procedures required by the institution. Remember that the performance appraisal is confidential information. It should be kept in a safe place and should be part of the employee's personnel file.

Follow up on the formal appraisal. Training or development programs may result from the interview. Set time frames for measuring performance improvement. Follow the formal review with regular informal reviews to monitor progress on improvements.[7]

Sample Evaluation Forms

Below are sample evaluation forms that reflect some different approaches to formal evaluation. They are used here to demonstrate various aspects of evaluation and are not considered models to be used necessarily as is.

Facing one's own strengths and weaknesses and articulating them is difficult for some people, but it can be the most effective form of evaluation.

It involves the person being evaluated not only in a response to a supervisor's observations but also in developing a conscious picture of himself or herself as part of a team and acknowledging the contributions one is making to the team effort and ideas for future productivity. The self-evaluation form in figure 1 is a simple, nonthreatening example. It starts from a positive position ("Most important job-related activities I do well") and avoids negative language by using the terms "Goals, ways to develop, and/or special projects for upcoming year." This type of form involves a minimum of writing and leaves most of the evaluation to an open-ended, face-to-face discussion with the written comments as jumping off points. It is probably the simplest, most casual form of formal evaluation, relying more on what is said than on what is committed to writing. It also has the advantage of fitting every position from administrator to page. It may be inadequate, however, when a staff member's performance requires close monitoring or disciplinary action. Such a simple form will necessitate other documentation to demonstrate unsatisfactory job performance.

Figure 2 is another general, open-ended evaluation form. This "Performance Contract" is designed as a self-evaluation, giving the staff member the opportunity to identify strengths and to recognize areas that need improvement as goals to be accomplished over the short and long term. Requiring the staff member to come up with a plan of action to accomplish the goals gives her or him a sense of investment in the process and the assurance that what is required is not beyond her or his capabilities.

Most libraries probably use a more detailed form than either of these. In all likelihood, a ranking system of some sort will be part of the written evaluation. Figure 3 represents a form that allows for a ranking of various components of job performance along with space for open-ended comments. Again, it is general and can be used for every job in the library. One drawback, however, is that it does not allow space for the person being evaluated to make any comments.

Some libraries may decide that the same evaluation form is not suitable for all job descriptions. Figures 4 through 7 show two different evaluation forms, one for librarians and senior clerical staff and one for clerical, custodial, and page staff. Figure 4 represents the cover sheet, which is the same for both. Note that not only does it have a space for the staff member to comment, but it also provides space for the employee to identify abilities or interests that are not being used in the present job.

Figure 5 represents the ranking portion of the form for professional staff. The use of "commendable" and "effective" as two ranking categories is a welcome departure from the usual language of evaluation, as are some of the descriptions of the performance standards.

Figure 6, which appears on both forms, provides for a numerical ranking of performance of specific duties of the job that are to be filled in for each position.

Finally, Figure 7 gives a list of standards for clerical, custodial, and page positions and a mechanism for grading performance.

These forms strike a good balance between structure and open-endedness and are neither too cumbersome nor too casual for managing evaluation of a sizable staff.

Complete prior to your evaluation to help your supervisor analyze your performance. This is voluntary. Fill it in if you wish and if you feel it will make your evaluation more meaningful.

Name _____ Department _____

Supervisor or Person (or persons) most appropriate to review form:

_____

Most important job-related activities I do well:

1. _____

2. _____

3. _____

Comments: _____

Comments on last year's performance plan (copy attached): _____

_____

_____

Goals, ways to develop, and/or special projects for upcoming year:

1. _____

2. _____

3. _____

Comments: _____

_____

_____

_____

Supervisor's/Director's Comments: _____

_____

_____

_____

FIGURE 1.   Self-Evaluation Form

Name _____ Date _____

Accomplishments (since last evaluation/approximately 1 year/be specific)

    1. _____

    2. _____

    3. _____

    4. _____

    5. _____

    6. _____

Goals

    Short-term

    1. _____

    2. _____

    3. _____

    Long-term

    1. _____

    2. _____

    3. _____

Plan of action (how you are planning to accomplish the above goals)

Please use the back or another sheet of paper if necessary.

Signature of Employee _____

Signature of Supervisor _____

FIGURE 2.   Performance Contract

Date _____

Return to Personnel by _____

Name _____

Assignment or Working Title _____ Department _____

Appointment (6 mos.) _____ Transfer _____ Annual _____

Other _____

If item is not applicable, place an asterisk (*) before the item number.

JOB PERFORMANCE	Superior	Excellent	Satisfactory	Below Standard
1. Amount of work performed	[ ]	[ ]	[ ]	[ ]
2. Accuracy	[ ]	[ ]	[ ]	[ ]
3. Organization of work	[ ]	[ ]	[ ]	[ ]
4. Judgment	[ ]	[ ]	[ ]	[ ]
5. Communication (oral & written)	[ ]	[ ]	[ ]	[ ]
6. Meeting and handling the public	[ ]	[ ]	[ ]	[ ]
7. Knowledge of position	[ ]	[ ]	[ ]	[ ]

PERSONAL				
8. Initiative	[ ]	[ ]	[ ]	[ ]
9. Flexibility	[ ]	[ ]	[ ]	[ ]
10. Attitude toward criticism	[ ]	[ ]	[ ]	[ ]
11. Cooperativeness	[ ]	[ ]	[ ]	[ ]
12. Relations with fellow workers	[ ]	[ ]	[ ]	[ ]
13. Self-confidence	[ ]	[ ]	[ ]	[ ]
14. Punctuality	[ ]	[ ]	[ ]	[ ]
15. Personal conduct	[ ]	[ ]	[ ]	[ ]
16. Health	[ ]	[ ]	[ ]	[ ]

SUPERVISORY ABILITY (When applicable)				
17. Planning and assigning	[ ]	[ ]	[ ]	[ ]
18. Training and instructing	[ ]	[ ]	[ ]	[ ]
19. Evaluating performance	[ ]	[ ]	[ ]	[ ]
20. Fairness and impartiality	[ ]	[ ]	[ ]	[ ]
21. Approachability	[ ]	[ ]	[ ]	[ ]
22. Leadership	[ ]	[ ]	[ ]	[ ]

FIGURE 3. Personnel Evaluation

Comments (By immediate supervisor)
  (Use additional sheet as needed—include specific comment on overall potential of
  each individual rated.)

Comments (By appropriate second supervisor)
  (Use additional sheet as needed)

Signature_____ Date _____

I have received a copy of this report and discussed it with the supervisor.

Employee's Signature _____ Date _____
  (Signature indicates opportunity to see and discuss. It does not necessarily connote
  agreement with contents.)

Evaluation (To be completed by immediate supervisor)

Overall Performance

  Superior _____ Excellent _____ Satisfactory _____ Below Standard _____

This report is based on my observation and/or knowledge. It represents my best judgment
  of the employee's performance.

Supervisor _____ Position _____ Date _____

Assistant Director _____ Date _____

Director _____ Date _____

Name _____ Date _____

Position _____ Time in Position _____ Last Review Date _____

Type of Report: Probationary _____   6 Month _____   Annual _____   Other _____

Present Supervisor _____ Period Covered _____

If employee has any special abilities or interests which are not being used on present job, briefly outline:

_____

_____

_____

Signatures and Comments

Supervisor

_____

_____

_____

_____

_____

_____

_____

Supervisor's signature _____

Staff Member

_____

_____

_____

_____

Staff member's signature _____

I have reviewed this report and I have been given the opportunity to discuss it with the Director. My signature does not necessarily mean that I agree with the report.

FIGURE 4. Evaluation Form

	Commend-able	Effective	Requires Improvement	Unsatis-factory	Does not Apply
A. General					
Employee regularly reports to work, returns from lunch or breaks and relieves other staff members promptly.					
Employee is tactful and courteous with co-workers and with the public.					
Employee's standards in dress and grooming enhance the image of the library.					
Cooperates with co-workers to create and preserve harmony and understanding in the work environment.					
Adheres to policies established by Library Board of Trustees and Administration.					
B. Organization and Administration					
Adheres to, interprets, and enforces library policy as necessary.					
Sets deadlines and submits reports and proposals that are complete, accurate, and on time.					
C. Professional Behavior					
Interprets library goals and programs to the public and promotes constructive relationships between the library and community.					
Keeps immediate supervisor informed of programs and activities related to assigned areas of responsibility.					
Demonstrates growth in scholarship and in professional expertise related to position.					
D. Leadership Skills					
Shows judgment, initiative, and creativity required of a person in this position.					
Presents clear, concise oral and written communications.					

FIGURE 5.   Ranking

Duties	Knowledge	Quality	Comments

Exceeds Requirements = 3   Meets Requirements = 2   Needs Improvement = 1   Unacceptable = 0

FIGURE 6.   Numerical Ranking

Disciplining Negative Performance

In all likelihood, if you are effectively practicing ongoing evaluation, the occasion for disciplinary action against an employee will seldom arise. Each negative incident will be promptly addressed and corrective measures put into place right away. But there still may come a time when a staff member's performance is so consistently poor that removal is the only recourse. It helps if the library has set up a step-by-step procedure for such situations, but, whatever the procedure, it will require accurate written documentation of negative performance over time. Figures 8–10 represent some examples of critical incident reports. They take the form of memoranda, and in each one the incident is clearly and concisely described. Figure 8 describes a one-time infraction and ends with a confirmation of the employee's past good record, implying the expectation that this isolated incident will not be repeated. (While in most libraries a one-time infraction by an employee with a good record would not be reprimanded in print, such a step might be taken if there is some expectation that it will happen again. This letter represents the first written reprimand, although verbal corrections may have preceded it.)

Figure 9 documents to a higher authority a conversation between a supervising librarian and a staff member concerning two incidents of tardiness.

	Excellent	Satisfactory	Improvement Needed	Unacceptable
Employee can be relied upon to complete jobs and deadlines without need of follow-up.				
Employee regularly reports to work, returns from lunch and breaks, and relieves other staff members promptly.				
Employee is tactful and courteous with co-workers and with public.				
Employee's standards in dress and grooming enhance the image of the library.				
Employee cooperates with co-workers to create and preserve harmony and understanding in the work environment.				
Employee adheres to policies established by Library Board of Trustees and those expressed in union contract.				
Employee avoids development of backlogs or alerts supervisor when this condition begins to occur.				
Employee anticipates potential needs and suggests appropriate actions to supervisor.				

FIGURE 7. Standards

January 10, 1994

MEMORANDUM

TO: Jane Doe
FROM: Supervisor's Name

On Thursday, January 3, 1994, you left the building without authorization during your scheduled work time. As you know, breaks must be taken on library premises unless you have been granted prior permission to leave the building by your supervisor. In addition, your break exceeded the fifteen minute allotment and extended to nearly thirty minutes. This reflects an inaccurate record of the time worked indicated by your punches. The payroll sheet taken from time clock must represent the actual time worked. Misrepresentation of time worked is a serious infraction.

Considering your length of employment and your good work performance, a letter of reprimand will be the only disciplinary action taken.

_____
Employee

_____
Supervisor

FIGURE 8.   Memorandum 1

November 23, 1994

MEMORANDUM

TO: Supervisor's Name
FROM: Librarian's Name
SUBJECT: Jane Doe

On Friday, November 22, 1994, I spoke with Jane Doe regarding her tardiness on 10/15/94 and 11/1/94. I told her she would need to be more aware of the time. I explained that she was required to be at her work station at the start of her shift. She indicated that she would allow more time for travel to prevent further tardiness.

_____
Employee

_____
Supervising Librarian

_____
Supervisor

FIGURE 9.   Memorandum 2

November 4, 1994

MEMORANDUM

TO: Jane Doe
FROM: Supervisor's Name

On November 1, 1994, you did not report for your assigned schedule at the Branch. You were scheduled to work from 9:00 a.m. to 1:00 p.m. You called the Branch at 11:00 a.m. and spoke with Alice Jones. You then called the main building and spoke with Betty Bee.

This is not proper procedure. When you are absent from work, you are required to notify your supervisor at the main building. If your own supervisor is not present, you are required to report to the supervisor assigned to duty at that time.

Any deviation from your assigned work schedule will result in further disciplinary action.

_____
                                                        Employee

_____
                                                        Supervisor

FIGURE 10.   Memorandum 3

Figure 10 is a combination critical incident report and statement of proper procedure for this situation. It ends with a warning. Seldom will any further action be necessary. Usually an employee will correct the negative behavior, particularly if his or her job or an expected salary increase is at stake. It is at this point that we can see how attitude needs to be formally addressed because it affects both individual performance and the smooth running of the department.

Relatively minor infractions are used in these three examples so as to focus more easily on the form, rather than the content, of the documentation. More serious incidents, perhaps involving higher level staff, would most likely be described in greater detail. The main point here is that these are written records of negative behavior that, taken together or with other documentation, may lead to termination. Note that these reports provide a place for both the employee and the supervisor to sign, indicating that both agree on the description of the event or events that necessitated the written action. If the employee disagrees or refuses to sign the report, the conference can be repeated with a third, neutral party present. That third person can sign the report as a witness to the conversation that took place between the supervisor and the employee.

Evaluating the Evaluator

We've discussed the value of a spirit of trust in the department as a key to successful ongoing performance evaluation. If this spirit exists, it is a foregone conclusion that the formal evaluation will be a fair appraisal, but it is still important to recognize some pitfalls to avoid when preparing the written evaluation. In her article "Conducting Performance Evaluations," Lucy R. Cohen describes eight ways to ruin a performance review:

1. Halo Effect—the supervisor gives a favorable rating to all position responsibilities based on impressive performance in one job function.
2. Pitchfork Effect—the opposite of the "halo effect," the supervisor gives a poor rating to all position responsibilities based on poor performance in one job function.
3. Central Tendency—the supervisor rates everyone as average, thereby avoiding making judgments.
4. Loose Rater—the supervisor rates everyone highly (this type of rater can also be called spineless or lenient). The supervisor thus avoids conflict by not pointing out weaknesses.
5. Tight Rater—the supervisor rates everyone poorly because he feels no one can live up to his standards.
6. Recency Error—the supervisor relies on recent events to determine a staff member's performance rating rather than the full period under review.
7. Length of Service Bias—the supervisor assumes that a tenured staff member is performing well because of his experience.
8. Competitive Rater—the supervisor determines a staff member's rating based on how he has been evaluated by his own supervisor.[8]

While it is unlikely that we would succumb to these pitfalls, knowing to avoid them can help us to develop fair, effective evaluations of those we supervise.

Conclusion

Few of us will ever list formal evaluation of our staff as one of our favorite duties, but the process can be productive and even rewarding when it is done properly. When youth services personnel are working to their full potential, when their good performance is acknowledged and compensated, when problems are handled and solved rather than ignored, the end result will be reflected in excellent service to the public we serve.

Notes   1. Charles R. McClure et al., *Planning and Role Setting for Public Libraries: A Manual of Options and Procedures* (Chicago: American Library Association, 1987).

2. Virginia A. Walter, *Output Measures for Public Library Service to Children: A Manual of Standardized Procedures* (Chicago: American Library Association, 1992).

3. Association for Library Service to Children, *Competencies for Librarians Serving Children in Public Libraries* (Chicago: American Library Association, 1989).

4. Ibid., 3.

5. James Jenks, "Personnel ReadyWorks," *Communication Briefings* 12, no. 3 (January 1993):1.

6. Joan Giesecke, ed., *Practical Help for New Supervisors* (Chicago: American Library Association, 1992), 22.

7. Ibid., 23–24.

8. Lucy R. Cohen, "Conducting Performance Evaluations," *Library Trends* 38(1) (Summer 1989):41–42.

Bibliography

Association for Library Service to Children. *Competencies for Librarians Serving Children in Public Libraries.* Chicago: American Library Association, 1989.

Cohen, Lucy R. "Conducting Performance Evaluations." *Library Trends* 38(1) (Summer 1989):41–42.

Giesecke, Joan, ed. *Practical Help for New Supervisors.* Chicago: American Library Association, 1992.

Jenks, James. "Personnel ReadyWorks," *Communication Briefings* 12, no. 3 (January 1993):1.

McClure, Charles R., Amy Owen, Douglas L. Zweizig, Mary Jo Lynch, and Nancy A. Van House. *Planning and Role Setting for Public Libraries: A Manual of Options and Procedures.* Chicago: American Library Association, 1987.

Walter, Virginia A. *Output Measures for Public Library Service to Children: A Manual of Standardized Procedures.* Chicago: American Library Association, 1992.

Chapter 11

Conducting Effective Meetings

Mary Fellows

Meetings are inescapable. They are part of our work, social, and sometimes even home lives. Meetings are the way in which groups of people get things done, and in our democratic society and egalitarian profession, they are a necessary part of nearly every week, if not every day. Why, then, do most of us inwardly, or if we are less inhibited, outwardly groan when we are informed of another meeting?

Generally, we groan because we believe that we are going to have to spend several hours wasting our time. In this age in which our smallest commodity is time, people resent spending hours on activities that do not seem to be productive, whether at work or outside it. Nonproductive meetings are costly, not only in employee satisfaction, but in salary for the employees involved who could be doing other things, goals not met because of time spent, and the costs of the meeting itself.[1] Your image as a leader can also suffer from bad meetings, and continually frustrating experiences can hurt staff morale.

A good meeting, on the other hand, can be extremely profitable, resulting in better decisions, higher morale, increased productivity, and stronger working relationships. To most wisely and effectively use the library's resources, a good manager must learn to conduct only necessary and productive meetings.

The first step in becoming an effective meeting conductor is to determine whether one is actually necessary. The broad reason for holding a meeting is to accomplish something. Any of the following may be accomplished:

Provide information

Gather input or data

Train

Inspire

Plan

Solve problems

Resolve conflict

Set goals

Evaluate progress toward goals

However, depending on the scope of the information to be provided, or the severity of the problem to be resolved, or the character of any of the other tasks, a meeting may not be necessary. Perhaps a report or a summary of statistical data might convey the information to be communicated more concisely. A memo to the staff or a letter to an individual might be just as effective in accomplishing the objective. Possibly a telephone call or a face-to-face conversation would solve the problem without involving others in a formal setting. Before calling a meeting, it is important for youth services managers to consider other options. Here's a good question to ask yourself: Is a meeting absolutely necessary to accomplish the end result that I need? If the answer is no, do not call one.

Preparing for the Meeting

What, Who, When, Where

Once it has been determined that a meeting will accomplish the job most effectively, you must formalize your objectives for the meeting. From the objectives stem decisions about who should participate, what format the meeting will follow, and when and where the meeting will be held.

In setting objectives for the meeting, it is important to be realistic. Consider the amount of information to be communicated or the magnitude of the planning to be done. If necessary, break the topic into smaller segments that can be more efficiently covered over a series of meetings rather than in one marathon. Our capacity for unbroken concentration is about one and one-half hours, and exercising a realistic view of employees' ability to learn new material, even if it means taking four days instead of one to present a change, is preferable to turning them into glassy-eyed zombies who will dread every future summons to a meeting.[2]

Once the objectives are in place, decide who absolutely needs to be there. In considering individuals to be included, the best process is to assess their knowledge of the subject to be discussed, their likelihood of being directly and significantly affected by the expected outcome, their position in the library or department, and their leadership among the rest of the staff.[3] Generally speaking, the smaller the group, the more efficient the meeting process. If there does not seem to be a reason for an individual to be involved in the meeting, do not include her or him. We have all sat in meetings wondering why we were there and wishing we were elsewhere. Try to communicate why the person is being included when she or he is invited to attend the meeting. Also, be sensitive to the person who thinks he or she should have been invited and was not; an explanation may smooth things over.

Next, consider the format of the meeting. Assuming the youth services manager will conduct the meeting, who else will have responsibility for presenting certain segments? Involve participants whenever possible. Not only does this provide variety in speakers, but it makes the process of informing seem more like a sharing of information than a delivery of the Ten Commandments by the Almighty. Involving others in the planning of the meeting as well as the actual presentations spreads some of the responsibility around and creates a stake in achieving the desired meeting results among the participants.[4]

Deciding where and when the meeting will be held is the next step. If the number of participants is small, take into account the schedules of the people you are inviting. If you are expecting a large group, try to discover if there are any major conflicts and avoid them. Let the staff members you are inviting know what time the meeting will start and approximately when it will end. If you do not know how long the meeting will take, pick a time anyway and resolve to end then and schedule another meeting if necessary. Employees appreciate a boss who respects their ability to manage their own time and gives them the information they need to do that.

When choosing a site for the meeting, think about what you want to accomplish and what feelings you need to engender to accomplish your objectives. Kieffer advises considering the comfort of your meeting partners, the image you would like to convey, and the advantages you may create for yourself by using location to your benefit.[5] For example, meeting in your office gives you a certain psychological advantage and allows you to be either hospitable or dominating depending on whether you need to counsel an employee or reprimand one. On the other hand, a meeting on a touchy subject at which you want a free exchange of ideas would be better held in a more neutral space, such as a board room or a place off-site.

The Agenda

Once the major decisions of why, who, when, and where have been made, communicate these decisions to the participants, and if appropriate, supply them with an agenda. This is key. Many meetings fail because of a lack of a known agenda. In general, the written agenda is crucial to any meeting that involves more than three people and more than three tasks. Kieffer identifies four uses of the agenda: first, it is a tool to aid in preparing for the meeting. Second, it communicates to participants in advance what items will be considered and what is expected of them. Third, the agenda is a script for the meeting itself and a means to control what happens in it. Last, it is a standard by which the meeting's success or failure may be measured.[6]

Basic items to include in the agenda are the time the meeting will begin, the time it will end, the purpose of the meeting, a list of participants, and pertinent written materials. But building a complete agenda actually requires an ability to work backward. Jeffries and Bates relate a method used by mystery writers—plotting the ending, and then working backward —and suggest its adaptation to preparing agendas. Pretend the meeting has just ended and the participants are leaving. What message are they taking with them, and how do they feel about that message?[7]

The structure of the agenda is also an important factor in the success of a meeting. A three-part agenda—informational, decisional, and discussional—allows participants to "warm up" gradually to major decisions and afterward to "cool down" with items simply meant for discussion. By giving people a chance to relax their attention slightly at the end, this process alleviates the problem of a participant whose viewpoint opposed the decisions made leaving the meeting still angry.[8]

One important point to remember in ordering the agenda is to keep the last or second-to-last item for new business. Given an early place in the agenda, new business can overpower the original agenda and leave participants feeling unprepared and taken advantage of. But used at the end of the meeting, a "you name it" section can bring to light problems and opportunities just cropping up, and allow you to choose to either handle it then and there if it is simple, or to commit to making it part of the next meeting's agenda.

Final Preparations

After you have decided on the agenda, distribute it within an appropriate amount of time before the meeting. The actual lead time depends on what you want to accomplish and how much preparation the participants must do ahead of time. Make preparation as easy as possible, but make it clear how much shorter the meeting will be if everyone involved actually does prepare. Also arrange in advance for the recording of actions, either by one of the attendees or by an outside person such as a secretary.

A last noteworthy point in preparing for a meeting is to attend to creature comforts. A good rule to remember here is "little things mean a lot." One new director who inherited a terrific team lost the goodwill of his new staff in part because he bought the cheapest possible donuts for the staff meetings. It seems a minor detail, but if an extra $3.00 buys you a little bit more of your meeting partners' goodwill, you're that much closer to realizing your meeting's objectives. Other creature comforts to consider include the light, ventilation and temperature in the room, and the rules regarding smoking.

Conducting the Meeting

To conduct a meeting most effectively, you have to be prepared both mentally—for the work that will be done at the meeting—and emotionally. Emotional preparedness is not a topic given a great deal of play, but it is important. If you are not ready emotionally for a meeting—if you resent either the time you will spend, having to deal with the topic in the first place, talking with the people involved, chairing the meeting, or any other aspect, your meeting will suffer. If you must be involved in a meeting about which you have qualms, take some time beforehand to do what it takes to psych yourself for it. Spend a few minutes away from the stress of the day to calm down, or list in your own mind any good things that could possibly come out of the meeting. But go into the meeting with at least a neutral, if not a positive, attitude. Particularly remember that when you are chairing the meeting, you set the tone. Do not allow your own negativity to sabotage the group.

In conducting the meeting, your role is not only that of a chairperson, but of a leader. Leading a meeting involves a number of elements. One of the first is to eliminate distractions. If you are holding the meeting in your office, ask whoever answers the phone to take messages for you, and communicate to your meeting partners that they should make the same arrangement. Make it clear to those it concerns that you are not to be disturbed, by instructing your secretary if you have one or by such nonverbal cues as closing your door. By taking the step of eliminating distractions you ensure a better chance of accomplishing your meeting objectives.

Acknowledge the schedules of the people you are meeting with by starting on time. This helps to set a businesslike tone and project an image of competence for you. Begin by welcoming your meeting partners or thanking them for making the time for the meeting, as appropriate. Get announcements out of the way quickly, then restate the objectives of the meeting and the estimated time. From there you should go through each point on the agenda, either covering the item yourself or moderating when others have responsibility for agenda items.

It is important that as the leader you control the meeting process, and this is why having an agenda is particularly valuable. The word "control" often is perceived to have negative connotations, but in the case of meetings it is really no more than managing the meeting process. Control is exercised by insisting that the group stay on task and by tactfully leading them back to the agenda when they get off track. If the discussion takes a turn toward gossip or similar unrelated information, suggest that the group continue discussing that particular topic at the break or during lunch.

A word of warning about the pitfalls of leading a meeting: be careful not to over control the process by imposing your own will on the group. If you called a meeting for a purpose other than strictly informational, it was purportedly because you sought your group's opinions. Allow them the opportunity to express and discuss their thoughts. A good meeting leader also knows that leadership may shift during the meeting among participants, which is fine. As Palmer and Palmer suggest, "The trick is to know *when* a leadership void is developing and *how* to jump in and fill the gap, either by providing the leadership or by encouraging others to do it."[9]

End the meeting when you said you would. Before doing so, summarize the outcomes of the meeting and relate those outcomes to your original meeting objectives. Preview what the next steps are, schedule the next meeting if necessary, and end on a positive note. Do your best to ensure that participants leave feeling that the meeting was worth their time and effort.[10]

After the Meeting

Distribute the minutes of the meeting to those involved shortly after the meeting. Minutes will serve as a refresher on decisions made and issues discussed when those items are no longer fresh in your mind and will also serve as a permanent record of what took place should that ever be called into question. Minutes also help clarify things that may not have been clearly understood and serve as a reminder of responsibilities assigned.

Evaluate the meeting, either by simply thinking about what took place and how you could have made things go more smoothly or by asking a participant you trust to give you some feedback on the event. Most of us are eventually able to learn from our mistakes, but we do not always recognize them right away.

Conclusion

Conducting effective meetings, like most skills, can be learned. The concepts to master are the ability to distinguish between necessary and unnecessary meetings, mental and emotional preparedness, respect for meeting partners, a healthy two-way flow of information, and good leadership skills. By increasing your proficiency in these areas and following the guidelines in this chapter, you can become an expert at conducting effective meetings.

Notes

1. Donald L. Kirkpatrick, *How to Plan and Conduct Effective Business Meetings* (Chicago: Dartnell, 1976), 22.

2. Marya W. Holcombe and Judith K. Stein, *Presentations for Decision Makers* (Belmont, Calif.: Lifetime Learning Publications, 1983), 150.

3. Kirkpatrick, *How to Plan,* 43.

4. Robert Maidment and William J. Bullock, Jr., *Meetings! Accomplishing More with Better and Fewer* (Reston, Va.: National Association of Secondary School Principals, 1985), 4.

5. George David Kieffer, *The Strategy of Meetings* (New York: Simon and Schuster, 1988), 184.

6. Ibid., 205.

7. James R. Jeffries and Jefferson D. Bates, *The Executive's Guide to Meetings, Conferences, and Audiovisual Presentations* (New York: McGraw-Hill, 1983), 66.

8. John E. Tropman and Gersh Morningstar, *Meetings, How to Make Them Work For You* (New York: Van Nostrand Reinhold, 1985), 59.

9. Barbara C. Palmer and Kenneth R. Palmer, *The Successful Meeting Master Guide* (Englewood Cliffs, N.J.: Prentice Hall, 1983), 124.

10. Kieffer, *Strategy of Meetings,* 242.

Bibliography

DeBruyn, Robert L. and James M. Benjamin. *Mastering Meetings.* Manhattan, Kans.: The Master Teacher, 1983.

Dunsing, Richard J. *You and I Have Simply Got to Stop Meeting This Way.* New York: AMACOM (A division of American Management Association), 1978.

Holcombe, Marya W. and Judith K. Stein. *Presentations for Decision Makers.* Belmont, Calif.: Lifetime Learning Publications, 1983.

Jeffries, James R. and Jefferson D. Bates. *The Executive's Guide to Meetings, Conferences, and Audiovisual Presentations.* New York: McGraw-Hill, 1983.

Kieffer, George David. *The Strategy of Meetings.* New York: Simon and Schuster, 1988.

Kirkpatrick, Donald L. *How to Plan and Conduct Productive Business Meetings.* Chicago: Dartnell, 1976.

Maidment, Robert and William J. Bullock, Jr. *Meetings! Accomplishing More with Better and Fewer.* Reston, Va.: National Association of Secondary School Principals, 1985.

Palmer, Barbara C. and Kenneth R. Palmer. *The Successful Meeting Master Guide.* Englewood Cliffs, N.J.: Prentice Hall, 1983

Tropman, John E. and Gersh Morningstar. *Meetings, How to Make Them Work for You.* New York: Van Nostrand Reinhold, 1985.

Chapter 12

Establishing Staff Relations

Kathy Toon

The key to all staff relations is good communication. Communication has been defined as "the interchange of thought or information to bring about mutual understanding and confidence or good human relations."[1] As a manager, the effectiveness with which you do or do not communicate sets the tone for your area of responsibility. In other words, the staff relations in your unit are determined in large part by your attitude and actions. Establishing good relations with and among staff often requires effort until it begins to come naturally. This discussion will focus on learning to build good working relations with the library staff above you, below you, at the same level, and staff in other departments or entities with whom you may wish to interact.

Types of Communication

Communication in organizations can be either formal or informal and may be said to be either vertical or horizontal. Vertical communication refers to the flow of information between supervisor and employee, while horizontal communication describes information flowing between peers. Formal communication downward usually comes in the form of written memorandums, policies, and procedures and is the method often used by upper management. Formal communication upward is often in the form of personnel recommendations such as promotions or merit raises, and responses to assignments from upper management.

Informal communication most often occurs horizontally and downward from supervisors to a work group. It may take the form of general conversation or just passing on new information, explanation of job responsibilities or assignments, and informal staff meetings. A common form of informal communication is the ever-present grapevine. Although the grapevine is sometimes considered negative, it can be a positive method of communication. It is fast, gives the staff an opportunity to participate in the information process, and is remarkably accurate. The grapevine takes on a more negative tone when it passes on false or harmful rumors. Good communication from above can sometimes control the grapevine, and it can be used by management to provide information to staff in an informal and nonthreatening manner.

Managers must remember that there are appropriate occasions for formal communication and appropriate occasions for informal communication, and wisely judge which is required. For example, description of a new policy on latchkey children should be communicated formally in a memo with all the details, so that staff members can refer back to the rules. However, a manager communicating formally in a memo that he or she is to be married would likely be viewed as cold.

Just as there are appropriate types of communication for diverse situations, there are also various ways to communicate with different people. Each person comes from a unique background and may interpret information differently. The manager should take care in all communication to use appropriate language for the intended audience to elicit the type of feedback desired. If feedback is lacking, or if there is a misunderstanding of something you have said, perhaps you need to rethink the way you are communicating.

Staff Relations

Relationships with staff follow in the same direction as the lines of communication. As a manager you must communicate with your supervisor, your peers, and the staff you directly supervise. Since most public libraries are a part of some type of governing body, you must also be able to form partnerships or networks with departments or entities other than the library. If you are in a branch library, a small library, or a large central library, someone cleans the building, maintains the grounds, services the computers, repairs air conditioning and plumbing, and provides security. It is equally important that we forge good relationships with these co-workers.

Opening and strengthening lines of communication both vertically and horizontally may require conscious effort on the part of the manager since a large segment of each day is spent in communicating at some level. George B. Lumsden provides an overview of what managers who make that conscious effort do for their employees:

> They give them assurance that what affects them and their jobs will be told to them as quickly and as accurately as possible.
>
> They make them feel part of a team—a company.
>
> They make them feel respected as individuals.
>
> They let them see their manager in the role of a helper on whom they can rely, and not just someone from whom they take direction.[2]

These are wonderful goals, but managers also need some practical ways to put communication theories into practice in our own libraries. Following are some ideas proven successful. How you use them will, of course, depend on the size of your library.

One of the staff relationships to develop particularly is that with your own supervisor. Your boss needs your support just as you need his or her support. The expression "It's lonely at the top," is a common one, and as a manager you too may sometimes feel that way. Your relationship with your supervisor will depend largely on your ability to communicate effectively. Staff members in each department in the library want to get their ideas heard by upper management, and it's important to learn how to be effective in this endeavor. There are several ways one might accomplish this:

Be truthful

Provide appropriate information to your boss's requests

Keep your boss informed so that he or she will not be surprised

Listen to your boss and learn to interpret his vision for your staff

Take responsibility for your problems

Learn what your boss wants and likes and then deliver

Provide service, quality, and results

Make your boss look good[3]

If you remember how you want those you supervise to respond to you, these points will be easy to remember.

Networking or forming liaisons within your library relies on good communication skills. Librarians as well as support staff should be encouraged or allowed to interact with other library service areas by cross-training, job rotation, committee assignments, or other library functions. Working in other areas of the library through cross-training or job rotation not only allows staff the opportunity to learn what service is provided by other departments, but it shows them how all areas of service fit into the library as a whole. The experience also provides the opportunity to form cooperative relationships with staff members throughout the library.

The phrase "walk a mile in my shoes" describes what cross-training can do for your staff. This is an easy way to develop good working relations within your organization. Whether a staff member assists at a central or branch library or in a public or technical services area, cross-training gives each staff member a better understanding and appreciation for the other's work. It is good for youth services librarians to visit with other youth services librarians in their own system if possible and also to work the adult services area. An appreciation for the technical services and circulation departments is also an important aspect of a youth services librarian's job. When you make an effort to get to know another's situation, he or she may react more favorably to your special needs.

Cross-training and job rotation can be practiced even with lower-level staff. During one hiring freeze, pages from other departments were borrowed to shelve materials and were rewarded by the children's page supervisor for their efforts. Another successful project involved summer reading programs. The pages in the children's department wanted to try their hand at a puppet show and a dramatic performance during the summer reading club. Word quickly spread through the building with the other young people, and several asked if they could participate. This provided an excellent cross-training opportunity for employees who are usually not allowed this opportunity. The performance was followed with a cast party for the pages involved, their supervisors, and managers.

Library committees or task forces are another way to develop networks for the manager and the staff. If possible, it is often advantageous to have a broad mix of experience on a committee. This is particularly true if the committee's charge affects the library as a whole. In an effort to select and implement a new automation system, for example, our library recently formed an automation task force. Any staff member who was interested in participating in the planning of this process was invited to do so. Consequently, the task force was made up of all staff levels from both the central library and branch libraries. This process provided staff who don't normally work together the opportunity to interact on a project that was mutually beneficial. The end result should be new liaisons formed for other communication opportunities.

Library functions, other than committees or task forces, that involve everyone offer another avenue to become better acquainted with staff from all areas of the library. Staff associations are an excellent way to provide social gatherings. If your library is large enough, a newsletter might also provide employees with informal information. An annual library book sale can bring all staff together from the director down to work with community volunteers to price, pack, load, unpack, and sell discarded library materials. This is truly a total library effort, and provides a tremendous opportunity to develop rapport with staff members from all levels and all areas of the library.

Another strategy for promoting staff interaction can be borrowed from the business community. Meals are often used by business people to court a client or make a deal. Eating together puts everyone on the same level and may serve as an icebreaker for discussions. One of the practices that has been very successful in cementing good communication and rapport between departments in some libraries is lunches. What may start out as lunch with another small department in an adjoining office area can grow to include people from all over the central library building. "Theme" lunches complete with decorations may be developed, along with conversation with staff from the business office, the word processing area, circulation, personnel, administration, computer support, exhibit department, and other subject departments. A wonderful opportunity can be provided not only for staff from diverse departments to get to know each other, but for clerks and pages to lunch with the director or assistant director. If you do this you may find that when you have a problem to be resolved with one of these departments, you already have an informal relationship established, which helps break the ice.

In addition to cross-training, job rotation, and cooperating on various library functions and events, courtesy is another important aspect of communication leading to networking with other staff. The importance of rewards and a simple thank you to other staff who help out with youth services cannot be stressed enough. When the director gives a story hour for summer reading club, follow up with a thank you from the staff. When another department loans a staff member for a special program, always reciprocate with time on one of their projects or a treat for their department. It is amazing what a batch of homemade cookies or a cake will do. When building collections for two new branch libraries, another branch manager and I furnished cookies for the technical services staff. They were delighted with our gesture, and we were grateful for their hard work.

Networks can also be formed with the other departments in your governmental structure, and it is important to build a base of contacts within this structure. Youth services librarians are naturals for fostering these cooperative relationships, and programs are a common link in this type of relationship. Fire and police departments are especially suited for children's programs in libraries. Some managers encourage the police who regularly patrol their neighborhood to stop by the library for their coffee break. If you do work with other departments on major projects, invite them to your next celebration. If they are included in the reward session too, your next cooperative endeavor will often be accepted more graciously. The benefit to you as the manager is a new professional friend and an opportunity to highlight the library to other departments.

These methods are not designed to get people to do what you want them to do or to bribe them. They need to be genuine means of thanks, and a means of becoming better working partners. Everyone works better for a common cause when they feel appreciated and valued as a person. As a supervisor, you are responsible for making your staff feel that they are important in their own work, and when you involve another department or section of your library in a children's project, you should do the same for them.

The majority of your communication and the bulk of developing staff relations will be downward from you to those whom you supervise on a daily basis. Good communication, teamwork, and courtesy are the keys to your success. One simple strategy is to treat your staff or co-workers as you would like them to treat you. For example, learn to make employees feel important. All employees need to know that they and their work are valuable to you and to the organization. Each of us wants to feel as if our work is valid, and we are making a contribution.

Communication in your work unit will probably be informal for the most part. Again, personnel actions will be the most formal part of unit communication. Staff meetings are a common way to handle the relay of information to all staff. In one very busy branch library the manager held informal staff meetings each morning by calling all of the staff to the break room for a coffee break about fifteen minutes before the library opened. At this time she read any memo that had arrived in the interoffice mail or shared with us any other information she might have received from another source. The staff at that particular branch felt like they were part of the whole library system and knew what was going on across the city. This was one of the most important things that this manager did to make the staff in that branch function as a team. They got to know each other well, and they came to know where their jobs fit into the whole system.

Your success as a manager is directly related to the people with whom you work. Friendliness is an element in managing that is used frequently by effective managers and seldom by ineffective managers. By using the term friendliness it is not suggested that you be your employees' best friend, lend them money, let them do what they want, or forgive poor job performance. Friendliness means the things you do that could be classed as courtesy, such as

Greeting people with good morning or good afternoon

Using please and thank you

Giving staff your undivided attention

Listening to what they say and not lecturing

Avoiding sarcasm

Apologizing if you are late or interrupt a meeting[4]

Since creating a comfortable working environment is part of your responsibility, another way to improve relations with your staff is to develop your ability to empower yourself and others. Lynda McDermott explains that "empowering others means creating a work environment in which people feel confident, secure, and fully capable of working and contributing at their full potential. It means removing obstacles and treating people in such a way they feel valued and respected. When people feel empowered, they are energized, motivated, and committed to both the organization and the person doing the empowering."[5] Empowerment lets employees use their own judgment, skills, and information to make decisions. Perhaps these hints will assist you in this process. You might allow your staff to participate in goal setting, let them suggest different ways to accomplish a task, ask for their help, give positive reinforcement and feedback, delegate, listen, give them clear instructions and let them know your expectations, show them that you trust them, encourage them to learn from mistakes, and provide opportunities for them to develop their skills.[6]

Every manager wants his or her work unit to function as a team. To develop a team spirit and encourage individuals to perform as a group, there are several things a manager can do. First you should understand the informal social structure of your group. Be aware of the needs of your employees and create a work environment where they can achieve job satisfaction as well as one that encourages cooperation. Let your employees know what you expect from them and then give them appropriate recognition and feedback based on merit. As the supervisor you need to be approachable and flexible in your leadership style. Let your staff know that you are interested in their welfare and development. Stand up for your staff when they are right and encourage them to learn from their mistakes when they are wrong. Rotating job assignments can create a team identity by removing some of the ownership of some job duties. As the manager you should have realistic expectations of your employees and build relationships that are based on mutual trust and respect.[7]

To get your group to work as a cohesive team, you must have an idea of how your work group functions both separately and together, and you must be able to identify the group dynamics. Building a team requires that the individual personalities and skills are blended to form a whole. Each person on the team must feel valued and necessary to the whole. When people get to know each other on a personal level, they develop a trust and comraderie. Some suggestions for creating an atmosphere for employees getting to know each other better are

> Going out on occasion with individuals or groups for lunch, coffee, or after work
>
> Putting employees who normally do not continually interact with one another on special projects and task forces
>
> Creating the time to talk about things of common interest
>
> Organizing a group picnic with families included
>
> Building cooperation through challenging activities
>
> Taking time out occasionally to talk with employees on a one-to-one basis[8]

Building a cohesive work group can only benefit you as the manager with the increased productivity and improved staff relations.

Even though you may have an excellent staff, personal problems at home or conflict between employees can often challenge the supervisor. Counseling and conflict resolution are perhaps one of the biggest challenges managers face. When an employee's personal life impacts the work place, counseling by the supervisor must take place. This is a skill that must be carefully used, and the supervisor's limitations must be recognized. A climate must be set by the supervisor that encourages the employee to discuss the problem that is affecting job performance. Listening skills are very important in this type of situation, as are tact and confidentiality. Through experiencing staff with a myriad of problems from mental illness, substance abuse, divorce, and domestic violence, managers quickly learn their limitations in the counseling process. Fortunately, many city governments offer a free counseling referral service to all employees through the personnel department. Supervisors may refer a troubled employee to this service, or the employee may contact them directly. If your library does not have that option available, another possibility is to check on whether the library's health plan covers counseling. If it does, offer to make an appointment for the employee with a qualified counselor, even rearranging his or her work schedule if necessary.

Conflict between employees can also cause problems in the work place. One strategy is to listen to each employee separately and try to obtain the full story before offering suggestions. Often if the employees in conflict sit down together and talk through their problem, they can resolve the conflict on their own. If this fails to resolve the issue, the manager may choose to serve as an arbitrator.

Communicating effectively and developing the type of staff relations necessary to build a cohesive work group in any organization requires much effort. The payback to the manager in smooth operations and a congenial work place is more than worth the effort.

Notes

1. Robert D. Stueart and John Taylor Eastlick, *Library Management,* 2d ed. (Littleton, Colo.: Libraries Unlimited, 1981), 145.

2. George J. Lumsden, *How to Succeed in Middle Management* (New York: American Management Association, 1982), 138.

3. Lynda McDermott, *Caught in the Middle* (Englewood Cliffs, N.J.: Prentice Hall, 1992), 100, 102.

4. Ferdinand F. Fournies, *Why Employees Don't Do What They're Supposed to Do and What to Do about It* (Blue Ridge Summit, Pa.: Liberty House, 1988), 94–95.

5. McDermott, *Caught in the Middle,* 99.

6. Ibid., 101.

7. Louis V. Imundo, *The Effective Supervisor's Handbook,* 2d ed. (New York: American Management Association, 1991), 52.

8. Ibid., 58–59.

Bibliography

Fournies, Ferdinand F. *Why Employees Don't Do What They're Supposed to Do and What to Do about It.* Blue Ridge Summit, Pa.: Liberty House, 1988.

Imundo, Louis V. *The Effective Supervisor's Handbook,* 2d ed. New York: American Management Association, 1991.

Lumsden, George J. *How to Succeed in Middle Management.* New York: American Management Association, 1982.

McDermott, Lynda. *Caught in the Middle.* Englewood Cliffs, N.J.: Prentice Hall, 1992.

Stueart, Robert D. and John Taylor Eastlick. *Library Management,* 2d ed. Littleton, Colo.: Libraries Unlimited, 1981.

Chapter 13

Networking and Cooperation

Melody Lloyd Allen

Public libraries are based on the value of sharing. Every preschooler attending story hour learns this lesson; every taxpayer contributes because of this philosophy; and every librarian should seek to expand services to citizens through a range of sharing efforts. Librarians can network with other librarians, other libraries, and other agencies within the community. In the end, any cooperation should benefit current or potential library users. In this chapter, examples have been drawn from personal experience, but the bibliography will lead you to many more projects from around the country.

Time, energy, resources, abilities, and attitudes will limit the extent and type of networking possible in providing library services to youth. Essential ingredients are the willingness of the youth services librarian and the support of administration. Allocations of staff, money, equipment, and materials, along with provision of any necessary training are all dependent on the library's priorities.

If the library has selected roles according to the process outlined in *Planning and Role Setting for Public Libraries,*[1] then overall priorities have been set as to whether the focus is on areas such as preschoolers, school support, or community activities. Whatever planning method the library has used to determine its roles in the community and its goals and objectives, these choices will affect service priorities and the level of networking that would support those priorities. All networking activities should be evaluated on the basis of their contribution to achieving objectives. Cooperative efforts are a means to an end; the end must be clear.

For instance, if the library has determined that a primary role is the Preschoolers Door to Learning, then much of the cooperation undertaken will be in conjunction with agencies serving preschoolers—nursery schools, Head Start programs, day care centers, and home day care providers. On the other hand, if the library has chosen to emphasize its role as a Formal Education Support Center, then the youth services librarian will devote more time and effort to working cooperatively with the schools both public and private. These roles and the subsequent goals and objectives affect decisions about whom the library works with as well as the level of effort to be expended.

Not only must a librarian consider why cooperation exists but also how it exists. Esther Dyer wisely points out:

> Cooperation solely on the level of interpersonal relationships is merely professional courtesy with the concomitant danger that, if the individuals change, the cooperative structure may well collapse. A personal, dynamic approach is laudable but should reflect policy, not substitute for it. While courtesy depends on individuals and can exist without policy support, coordination takes money and administrative backing.[2]

Examining more closely these structures and activities requires some clarification of terminology. Networks link the parties involved through a structure. Formal networks have stated and agreed to policies and procedures. Informal networks are more fluid and undefined. Both provide a structure before the immediate need for cooperation, yet are ready to be activated as a need arises. The most common example of a formal network is a group of libraries that have agreed to lend materials for interlibrary loan. They have in common a goal of providing materials for their users, and activate the network when a request is received for a specific item not in the collection. An informal network could be a group of librarians from neighboring communities who meet twice a year. At one gathering, they discover that they are all concerned about latchkey children and subsequently share their evolving policies.

Cooperative efforts involve working together on a specific project, whether this is done through an established structure or one created specifically to carry out the activity. Consider four possible levels of cooperation:

Liaison occurs when one party has a representative who is responsible for maintaining communication with the other party

Coordination occurs when one party has a goal and another party can assist in accomplishing that goal

Collaboration occurs when each party has a goal with some degree of overlap which leads to planning and together conducting a common activity

Partnership occurs when both parties share a goal and contribute and benefit on a more or less equal basis

The level of cooperation for a specific activity will vary according to its relationship to the library's priorities and the resulting allocation of resources, balanced with the degree of effort required to participate. Some cooperative efforts with limited connection to the library's goals are undertaken for the sake of creating "good will" when the level of effort is relatively low.

Cooperation should not be viewed as an "extra" but as a basic component of a good youth library service program. Youth services librarians must include in their repertoire the skills that underlie cooperation—skills in communication (oral, written, and conducting effective meetings), planning and evaluation, and advocacy for children. The competencies needed for effective library services for youth are clearly delineated in *Competencies for Librarians Serving Children in Public Libraries.*[3] Five of the seven sections contain items directly related to networking and cooperation, demonstrating the essential part cooperation plays in serving the information needs of children in the community (*see* figure 1).

Competencies Related to Networking and Cooperation

I. Knowledge of Client Group

    3. Assesses the community regularly and systematically to identify community needs, tastes, and resources.

    6. Understands and responds to the needs of parents, caregivers, and other adults who use the resources of the children's department.

    7. Maintains regular communication with other agencies, institutions, and organizations serving children in the community.

III. Communication Skills

    2. Demonstrates interpersonal skills in meeting with children, parents, staff, and community.

    4. Speaks effectively when addressing individuals as well as small and large groups.

IV. Materials and Collection Development

    C. Ability to Provide Patrons with Appropriate Materials and Information

        7. Maintains direct contact with community resource people so that children and adults working with children can be referred to appropriate sources of assistance.

V. Programming Skills

    3. Provides outreach programs commensurate with community needs and library goals and objectives.

    4. Establishes programs and services for parents, individuals, and agencies providing child care, and other professionals in the community who work with children.

VI. Advocacy, Public Relations, and Networking Skills

    4. Acts as liaison with other agencies in the community serving children.

    5. Develops cooperative programs between the public library, schools, and other community agencies.

FIGURE 1. Competencies for Librarians Serving Children in Public Libraries

Networks

Formal

Formal networks include city, county, regional, and state systems. Services include sharing resources and information and structures within which to cooperate on specific activities. Interlibrary loan, cooperative purchasing, information sharing meetings, continuing education, and public relations campaigns can help the youth services librarian offer better services by combining and broadening resources. Multitype networks can be especially effective in strengthening school-public library cooperation by moving beyond the individuals involved to institutionalizing certain types of cooperation. Formal networks may require a commitment to cooperation as a basis for membership.

Be sure to take advantage of all the services a network has to offer. Consultants at the state or system level providing technical assistance and grant funding are often available. Staff are accustomed to making referrals to others who may have experience with similar cooperative projects.

Informal Networks

Informal relationships among colleagues can also lead to resource and information sharing as well as cooperative projects, but they do not require establishment of governance, policies, and procedures; there may be simple rules and guidelines to make the contacts productive since this networking moves beyond friendships. Cooperation of all types can stem from or lead to valued friendships, but the needs of our clientele demand relationships sanctioned by the organization. A key ingredient of many informal networks, however, is emotional support.

Informal networks are particularly important for librarians in isolated situations such as one-person libraries and remote locations. When distance is not a factor, youth services librarians in a geographic area may meet on a regular basis to discuss problems and ideas. In Rhode Island, youth services librarians are fortunate to be able to meet together three times a year under the auspices of the state library agency. These sessions enable joint planning and problem solving. Afterward, it is always easier to contact someone you have met face to face than an unfamiliar name to whom you have been referred.

Problems with distance and staff coverage can now be partially overcome by electronic networking. The Library of Rhode Island (LORI) offers electronic forums or special interest groups, with one on children's services and another on young adult services. Sharing has involved ideas for booktalking, exchange of policies for public access computer use, answers for difficult reference questions, and development of bibliographies. Moral support was also given to a librarian coping with service reductions because of a budget crisis.

On a broader arena, electronic lists and computer-mediated conferences on a common interest allow for similar sharing and interchange. An example is PUBYAC, an electronic forum on public library services for young adults and children, which has witnessed debate over intellectual freedom issues as well as requests for identification of "that blue book I read in 1948 about. . . ." Both types of electronic networking mirror the informal gathering at a nearby library in that much of the valuable assistance gained is unanticipated but would not occur if this informal structure did not exist.

Also the level of participation in informal groups can vary over time and by individuals. These informal groups succeed in involving librarians with wide variety in their backgrounds and levels of experience. An "old hand" may offer pointers to a new librarian regarding discipline. The librarian just out of library school may be aware of new databases to aid in answering reference questions. One person may be strong in science activities, while another is acquainted with performers or continuing education presenters. Electronic forums allow anonymous, silent participation that the norms of actual gatherings might counter. As a professional, the librarian should acknowledge a responsibility to give as well as take in informal networks.

Library School

Your informal network will begin in library school or sooner if you have work experience before enrolling. Some programs facilitate this process, but at others where most students attend part-time, it can be difficult. Student organizations, small group work in class or for assignments, and social functions all encourage the development of networks. Driving to classes together in Rhode Island has formed many bonds that have lasted beyond graduation. A recent library school graduate contacted a former classmate when she faced a challenge from a parent to a title in her collection. Her colleague was able to assist by sharing her school system's collection development policy. Creating mini-reunions or attending school-sponsored ones at conferences renew these relationships.

Mentors are an important link in your network. Potential candidates are library school faculty and supervisors early in your career. Many beginners seek positions where they will work under the guidance of seasoned youth services personnel just so they can supplement the learnings from their course work with on-the-job training. Student internships or professional field placements can provide the same benefits. Mid-career librarians who serve as mentors are often energized by such relationships as well. They invite examination and analysis of professional values and experiences and encourage fresh perspectives. The mentor can pull away from the day-to-day responsibilities, sift through years of practice, and draw conclusions about what is important to share.

Professional Associations

Particpation in professional associations can be one of the most rewarding and pleasurable networking alternatives. Whether it is a state, regional, national, or international organization, the contacts can prove invaluable. Conferences offer continuing education, discussion forums, exhibits, and informal opportunities to talk with other librarians within and beyond a particular subject speciality. Poster sessions permit individuals to share research and accomplishments that often might never be published.

To get the most out of conferences, it is desirable to meet new people. Sit by a stranger at a meal, at a program, or on the bus; talk to an exhibitor whose services are unfamiliar; attend a program off the youth services "track"; seek out a roommate. Be sure to collect business cards and have some to hand out, as it is hard to remember names at the end of a long conference.

At large conferences, the experience will be enhanced by joining a committee or a discussion group of those interested in areas that concern you. Not only will you be able to make a contribution, but you will get to know a small group of people who will be part of your personal network. In fact, two of the members of the first committee I was appointed to in the American Library Association (ALA) have gone on to be presidents of the Association for Library Service to Children (ALSC) division.

Over a career, you will develop an extensive colleague group to draw on when need arises. As a result of my involvement with ALA, I have had calls from Hawaii about long-range planning, from Ohio about science fair resources, from Florida about public access computers, and from Vermont about running a mock Caldecott. From Vermont I received a core list of books for beginning readers, from Florida a newsletter that often lists information that I use in my own newsletter, from Ohio a Summer Reading Program manual on a theme similar to one in Rhode Island, and from Hawaii insight into the functioning of a statewide library system in another small state. My contact from Vermont has been a colleague-friend since library school, a long-standing member of my network.

Networks beyond the Library Community

There are also both formal and informal networks of youth-serving agencies, which strengthen the efforts of all the agencies in areas of youth advocacy, public relations, and alternate funding. In addition, library services can be delivered more effectively to segments of the community when done in conjunction with agencies that have acceptance and established clienteles within those segments of the community. Councils of youth service providers offer all levels of cooperation. The Newport (RI) Public Library participates in the Newport County Council of Community Services and the Newport Network for Children and Families. Through these structures, the library has been involved in cooperative efforts with Head Start, day care facilities, a shelter, and the Navy Base. Currently, the library is working with some of the agencies to establish homework support centers in the agencies.

As an example on the state level, the director of the state library agency in Rhode Island participates in the Children's Cabinet, a governmental organization that includes representation from state agencies serving children. They meet monthly to set policy, develop budget priorities, and discuss progress on interagency projects that involve children and families. Cooperation among Children's Cabinet agencies has included the development of grant proposals for family centers and the planning of services in support of a project to provide transitional housing for the homeless in former military housing.

Cooperative Efforts with Community Agencies

Numerous agencies in the community or state are concerned with youth and are potential allies in delivering library services to children and their families. The trend to provide social, educational, and health services to children in the context of the family has the potential to be both more challenging and more effective in the long term. This approach has made the library a natural partner for many agencies since the library has always worked with the whole family. For youth services librarians, it may require new attitudes, skills, and roles as consultant, trainer, and team member. For example, the youth services librarian might be called on to train early childhood educators who will subsequently train parents in ways to introduce books and book-related activities at their centers. Family literacy programs combine adult tutoring and reading motivation for children. Figure 2 suggests the range of agencies to consider working with cooperatively.

Following are examples of the four levels of cooperation with community agencies.

Liaison

The liaison's job is to keep open the channels of communication. Serving as a member of the board for a community agency is one example. As the public librarian in a neighborhood with several private schools, I attended the lower school librarians' meetings. The library's newsletter can be sent to schools and community agencies. This basic level of cooperation can

---

Preschools and Day Care Centers

Child Serving Agencies—Scouts, 4-H, Extension Programs

Arts and Cultural Organizations

Shelters and Group Homes

Hospitals

Recreation Programs

Professional Associations at the local level including the International Reading Association, the Association for the Education of Young Children, and the National Council of the Teachers of English

Family Literacy Programs

Commercial and Nonprofit Organizations

Juvenile Welfare Boards

FIGURE 2.   Community Agencies to Work with on Cooperative Efforts

help avoid scheduling conflicts; for example, the library and the recreation department can coordinate their summer calendars. Liaison work can also lead to identification of potential program presenters.

Coordination

Coordination means helping a group with their project. Setting up a library booth at a community or state fair is a case in point. In working with the Rhode Island Association for the Education of Young Children on the observance of the Week of the Young Child, the local zoo for a dinosaur exhibit, and with the Newspaper-in-Education Department of the *Providence Journal,* I developed bibliographies related to their projects. The Warwick Public Library has produced a newsletter for home day care providers with tips for working with young children.

Libraries can receive support from community agencies as well. The International Institute has translated flyers into several languages. A church in Tiverton made available a performance space for the final Summer Reading Program party. The Recreation Department in one community lists the library's summer events for children in the calendar it distributes to every town residence. When a local book store had a costumed book character for an appearance, they lent the costume to the library for story hour.

Collaboration

Collaboration involves some overlap in purpose that prompts two groups to work together. My concern as a public librarian to respond to the parents of toddlers in my two-year-old story hour who asked for information and referral about preschool programs, led me to talk with directors of nursery schools. Naturally, they were interested in recruiting enrollees. So together we planned a preschool program fair where a dozen nursery school and day care centers set up informational tables in the library during a February session of the story hour for two-year-olds. The local YMCA wanted to run a summer program; the library had a lot of kids hanging out with little to do. In the end, the library provided space, book deposits, and registered kids, while the Y provided leaders and activities.

The Providence Public Library has collaborated with Rhode Island Hospital so that children have positive reading motivation experiences, caring attention, and simply much needed distractions. Funding from the state helped to establish a deposit book collection for individual use and volunteer read-alouds. The library also sent staff to tell stories. The hospital provides space for the books and the storytelling as well as volunteers to read to children and circulate books.

In developing Rhode Island's Summer Reading Program, the librarians have wanted to offer children incentives to continue reading through the summer and complete the program. At the same time, the Children's Museum of Rhode Island (and subsequently other museums) was looking for ways to bring in new families. These goals brought the agencies together as Summer Reading Program participants received coupons for free admission to a different museum for each book read.

On a community level, the Johnston Recreation Department worked with the public library so that both could offer more performances during the summer. The Recreation Department provided funds for additional shows using a block booking rate available to the library. Then some of the shows were held in the library and others were held at one of the parks within walking distance of the library. The park could hold more people, taking advantage of the Recreation Department's stage and sound system, and attracted some people who did not normally attend library events.

Partnership

Partners work together on an equal footing sharing the same goals. The Rhode Island Children's Book Award is sponsored by the Rhode Island Library Association, the Rhode Island Educational Media Association, and the Rhode Island State Council of the International Reading Association. Three committee members come from each association. The chair and other positions rotate among associations as well as the financial responsibility for the project. All parties share the goal of promoting reading.

Women & Infants Hospital also cares about encouraging reading. It is part of maintaining their positive image in the community of caring about the families they serve to be perceived as a supporter of education. The library community under the auspices of the Department of State Library Services works with them to present the annual Rhode Island Festival of Children's Books and Authors, which gives children the chance to meet award-winning authors and have books autographed. More than three hundred at-risk children attend on scholarships distributed by agencies such as Big Brothers/Big Sisters and the hospital's adopted school. As well as sharing in the effort to achieve the goal of reading promotion, the partners share in a fund-raising goal. Proceeds benefit the hospital and further reading promotion projects in school and public libraries, such as the Summer Reading Program and the Rhode Island Children's Book Award.

Leap Into Literature was a three-year venture of Rhode Island public libraries, Old Stone Bank, and Duffy and Shanley (a public relations firm). Designed to bring history to life, the project brought four hundred shows based on books about people who had made a contribution in America to children at libraries throughout the state. When the bank became aware that there was little biographical material for elementary-age children on important Rhode Islanders, the culminating effort was the publication of a collective biography that was donated to libraries and showcased by the performers.

Encouragement to read can take place through partnerships within local communities. The Cranston Public Library has teamed up with the Chapter 1 teachers at a neighborhood elementary school and a local housing project to encourage at-risk children to maintain their reading skills over the summer vacation by bringing the Summer Reading Program to the housing project. The housing project provided space in the community room for a collection of books established by the library. Chapter 1 teachers promoted the program at the end of the school year and even visited during vacation. The librarian came once a week to share books and activities with the children and record their progress with the reading program. Parents kept the mini-library open at other times. All parties rated this cooperative effort as a great success that would not have been possible without the contributions of each of the parties.

Another example would be cooperative efforts between several libraries and the Red Cross to train adolescents as baby-sitters. Garden Clubs have joined libraries in guiding children in beautifying the area around the library. Senior citizens have benefitted along with children when they read aloud to them or teach them computer skills at the library.

On the national level, an evolving effort since 1989 is the Library–Head Start Partnership Project. It has developed a video and a resource notebook that can guide partnerships at the local level. One of the basic principles is that each agency can support the other to "enhance learning and parent involvement in children's literacy and language development."[4]

Cooperative Efforts with Schools

Finding ways for schools and public libraries to work together in providing effective library services for children within a community has proved a challenge frought with difficulties. Obstacles include inadequate staffing, lack of time scheduled away from classes, or need for a public service area for communication and planning, turf battles, competing for funds, and a limited vision of the potential benefits of cooperation. Young people can benefit the most from a team approach to providing a wide range of resources and services.

Following are examples of cooperation with schools.

Liaisons

Often this initial communication stage is the hardest barrier to overcome. It does not matter who takes the initiative, but someone must, and the youth services librarian at the public library generally has more freedom in terms of authority and scheduling. Initial contacts, however, must respect the chain of command so that the relationship will be institutionalized, not just personal.

Therefore, approval should be sought from the library director and permission granted from the Superintendent. A letter outlining the kind of contact you wish to make and closing with a statement that you will assume approval if there is no response by a reasonable time limit will suffice. Blanket permission obtained initially to distribute flyers from the public library and to visit classes will save a great deal of time and energy in the long run. In some school systems, permissions must also be granted by the principals. Finally, make the acquaintance of the school library media specialists and renew these annually in case there have been staff changes. Many problems can be avoided if all these contacts are made before there is a deadline looming for a specific cooperative effort.

A critical form of liaison communication is being informed of homework assignments in advance. In some cases, teachers do not warn the school library media specialist of upcoming major assignments let alone inform the public library. An "Assignment Alert" form can help (*see* figure 3). These can be distributed at a teachers' meeting at the beginning of the school year. Take advantage of this appearance to share tips regarding assignments: (1) when masses of kids have the same assignment, there just aren't enough materials to go around, (2) when use of encyclopedias is denied, some of the best sources of information on countries, animals, and scientific topics will be eliminated, and (3) when kids must read a book with more than one hundred pages, a lot of terrific books at grade level and all those books written just for third and fourth graders that are ninety-six pages long are eliminated.

Experience usually prepares the librarian for many assignments that repeat annually, such as reports on countries and science fair projects. As more schools move to literature-based thematic units, a librarian who is aware of the themes could send once or twice a year to the school an annotated list of new materials on these themes. Timely sharing of information on the latest winners of awards for children's literature and media is also appreciated. It is important that communication be a two-way street.

Coordination

Schools and public libraries can help each other through school visits. Classes can visit the public library in support of the teaching of library skills. Students receive an orientation to the library and can be introduced to specific materials. Such a visit is especially helpful when the school library media specialist would like students to be familiar with resources not available at the school. As in teaching any library skill, the visit will be most productive if students can apply it to work in which they are currently involved.

School libraries in Rhode Island have supported local public libraries by providing summer loans. Computers that otherwise would sit idle have been moved to the public library. In one community where the Summer Reading Program traditionally left empty shelves because of the limited size of the collection, the school allowed the library to borrow the beginning readers during July and August. The public library did not need nor did it have sufficient space for such a large collection in this area during the rest of the year.

Collaboration

The Library Power grants funded by the DeWitt Wallace-Reader's Digest Fund have promoted collaboration between school and public libraries in cities that have received them. While designed to improve school library media centers, public library staff in Providence have served on the advisory board, participated in workshops, and been consulted on collection development. The public library is aware that strengthening the services available through the school contributes to quality library services to the children of the community. The DeWitt Wallace Foundation recognizes the importance of school–public library cooperation and builds it in as a component of its grant awards.

Assignment Alert Form Grades K – 12 (Return this form to the public library)

School: Teacher: Telephone:
Grade Level: Class Size: Subject Area:

Types of Assignment

_____ Individual Projects   _____ Team Project   _____ Other

Project Requirements (Please attach handout students receive)

_____ Start Date   _____ Date Due   _____ Number of Pages
_____ Bibliography Required
_____ Number of Sources Required (books, magazines, etc.)
_____ Page Requirements for Books
_____ Other Requirements:

Special Requirements

_____ Atlas   _____ Magazines   _____ Costume   _____ Recipe
_____ Graphics (map, photos, portraits)
        (Please advise students about copyright and vandalism concerning photos)
_____ Globe   _____ Flag   _____ Project/Demonstration
_____ Other Special Requirements:

Additional Comments:

Assignment Alert Library Services
(Please check any you are interested in)

_____ Display   (A core collection of materials on a topic for your class
                     which may be checked out.)

_____ Post   (Assignment sheet, bibliography requirements, etc., posted
                     on our Assignment Alert bulletin board.)

_____ Book list   (Library staff will check a book list you send us for the
                     availability of titles related to the topic in this and nearby
                     libraries.)

_____ Quick Bib   (Library staff will locate or compile a quick bibliography on
                     the topic with ample notice.)

_____ Assistance   (Library staff will assist teachers with locating books to bor-
                     row on the teacher's card for in-class use.)

_____ Class Visit   (Schedule a library visit to begin researching a topic. Library
                     staff will highlight especially useful resources.)

_____ Booktalk   (Children's Librarian will visit upper elementary classrooms
                     to highlight especially useful resources, fiction, or a particu-
                     lar genre, i.e., award books, biographies, etc.)

FIGURE 3.   The Assignment Alert flyer distributed to teachers by Anne McLaughlin, children's librarian at the Champlin Memorial Library in West Warwick, Rhode Island, has an attractive front cover with an apple on top of a pile of books and a back cover with the library's address, phone number, and hours. The two critical sections shown here ask teachers about assignments and the use of library services.

Partnership

Several school and public libraries have pooled their resources and planning time to host joint author programs. The author appears during the day at the school and in the evening does a presentation for a family audience. In this way, each contributes to and benefits from the author's visit.

Conclusion

Networking and cooperation can enrich the services youth receive in a community. But in many ways, it would be a mistake to think that the library will save staff time and money. It has been my experience that building relationships, accessing the offerings of a network, and working on cooperative projects take more time than expected in communications and meetings. Working out respective roles and responsibilities and clarifying how tasks will be completed involve complex negotiations. Even the most proactive librarian will find that ongoing attention is needed for cooperative relationships.

It is so important, then, that each cooperative effort contribute to serving the information needs of youth. Those efforts and relationships that contribute to the knowledge, skills, and attitudes of the youth services librarian often have a more indirect, but substantial, effect on the youth services program. Positive public relations for the library as a concerned and involved community agency should be anticipated as a by-product of most cooperative efforts. That is why it is critical to follow through in a consistently professional manner.

Most often, the effort is worth it. Planning, implementation, and evaluation are enhanced. Varying perspectives enrich the final product. Ultimately, networks and cooperation evolve into a strong spiderweb that interconnects the library with an ever-expanding community of resources and agencies.

Notes

1. Charles R. McClure, et al., *Planning and Role Setting for Public Libraries* (Chicago: American Library Association, 1987).

2. Esther R. Dyer, *Cooperation in Library Service to Children* (Metuchen, N.J.: Scarecrow Press, 1978), 7.

3. Association for Library Service to Children, *Competencies for Librarians Serving Children in Public Libraries* (Chicago: American Library Association, 1989).

4. Virginia H. Matthews, et al., *Guide to the Use of the Library Head Start Partnership Video for Programs and Workshops* (Washington, D.C.: The Center for the Book, 1993).

Bibliography

Association for Library Service to Children. *Competencies for Librarians Serving Children in Public Libraries*. Chicago: American Library Association, 1989.

Benne, Mae. *Principles of Children's Services in Public Libraries*. Chicago: American Library Association, 1991.

Carlson, Pam. "Shining Stars: Public Library Service to Children in Shelters." *School Library Journal* 38, no. 7 (July 1992):18–21.

Connor, Jane Gardner. *Children's Services Handbook*. Phoenix, Ariz.: Oryx Press, 1990.

Del Vecchio, Stephen. "Connecting Libraries and Schools with CLASP." *Wilson Library Bulletin* 68, no. 1 (September 1993):38–40.

Denniston, Susan W. *Library Child Care Link: Linking Libraries with the Child Care Community*. South Bay Collaborative Library System, 1985.

Directions for Library Service to Young Adults, 2d ed. Chicago: American Library Association, 1993. 21–22.

Dyer, Esther. *Cooperation in Library Service to Children*. Metuchen, N.J.: Scarecrow, 1978.

Fasick, Adele M. *Managing Children's Services in the Public Library*. Englewood, Colo.: Libraries Unlimited, 1991.

Fox, Beth Wheeler. *The Dynamic Community Library*. Chicago: American Library Association, 1988. 14–19.

Haycock, Ken. "Networking—Essential to Survival" In *The School Library Program in the Curriculum,* 77. Englewood, Colo.: Libraries Unlimited, 1990.

Immroth, Barbara Froling. "How Is the Next Generation of Library Users Being Raised? The First National Survey on Services and Resources for Children in Public Libraries." *Public Libraries* 29, no. 6 (November-December 1990):339–41.

Kids Need Libraries: School and Public Libraries Preparing the Youth of Today for the World of Tomorrow. Chicago: American Library Association, 1990. Brochure. Reprinted from *School Library Journal,* April 1990.

McClure, Charles R., Amy Owen, Douglas L. Zweizig, Mary Jo Lynch, and Nancy A. Van House. *Planning and Role Setting for Public Libraries*. Chicago: American Library Association, 1987.

Rollock, Barbara. *Public Library Services for Children*. Hamden, Conn.: Library Professional Publications, 1988.

Semler, Duane and Mary Ann Walker. "Alternative Consultants—Colleague Networks, Internal Consultants and Peer Review." In *Using Consultants in Libraries and Information Centers,* 233–39. Westport, Conn.: Greenwood Press, 1992.

Smardo, Frances A. "Public Library Services for Young Children in Day Care and Their Caregivers." *Public Library Quarterly* 7, nos. 1–2 (Spring-Summer 1986):45–56.

"Youth Services Cooperating into the '90s." *Illinois Libraries* 72, no.2 (February 1990).

Contributors

Melody Lloyd Allen has worked in both school and public libraries, and, for the last fifteen years, at the Rhode Island Department of State Library Services. She has taught children's literature courses at the graduate library schools of University of Rhode Island and Simmons College and at the Center for the Study of Children's Literature at Simmons. She has served on several ALA committees and has been chair of both RILA's Intellectual Freedom Committee and the New England Round Table of Children's Librarians. The Rhode Island State Council of the International Reading Association awarded Allen the 1993 Literacy Award, reflecting many cooperative efforts.

Kathleen Deerr has twenty years of public library experience in Youth Services. Currently she is the head of Children's and Parents' Services at the Mastics-Moriches-Shirley Community Library. Deerr has served as an adjunct professor at the Palmer School of Library and Information Science and SUNY Stony Brook and is active in many local professional organizations. She has presented numerous lectures and workshops including using statistics to justify budget requests for the Nassau Library System. Her published works include the *Parent/Child Workshop: A Program Handbook* and articles in *Children's Video Report* and *Bookmark*. She has also contributed to many bibliographic publications including *Play, Learn and Grow*, published by Bowker.

Sherry Des Enfants is the Youth Services coordinator for the DeKalb County (Georgia) Public Library, and is an active member of ALA/ALSC. She is particularly concerned with developing and implementing services to reach children and families with special needs, an interest which has led her into the world of library fund-raising. Among her current projects are Project Horizons, which delivers library services to families in shelters (LSCA Title I grants, corporate and private sponsorship); Building Blocks to Literacy, which introduces teen moms and their very young children to early learning activities (Barbara Bush Foundation for Family Literacy grant); Building Blocks on Wheels, which reaches high-risk families (LSCA Title I grant); and Focus on Literacy, an adult and family literacy initiative (LSCA Title VI grant).

Floyd C. Dickman is the head of Library Development at the State Library of Ohio (Columbus). He has a B.S. in education from Miami University, Ohio, and an M.L.S. from the University of Michigan. He is the author of *Long Range Planning for Public Libraries* (revised edition, State Library of Ohio, 1988) and has served on numerous committees of the ALSC, including Caldecott, ALSC/Association of Booksellers for Children (Joint), and Preschool Services and Parent Education. Dickman is a member of the LAMA/John Cotton Dana Public Relations Award and consults on long-range planning, children's services, and children's literature.

Mary Fellows has a bachelor's degree in business administration and English from Augustana College (Sioux Falls, S.D.) and an M.L.S. from Indiana University. She has participated in the management process from both manager and employee perspectives in the retail, insurance, and library fields. Her recent library experience has included managing a busy youth services department in a suburban Chicago library; working in a large regional library system as a full-time consultant with youth services librarians on staffing, collection management, and organization issues; and administering a library in northwest Ohio. Fellows has been published in *School Library Journal,* and she is also the creator and author of the two-year-old *NORWELD Express,* a regional library system newsletter. She is currently director of the Weston Public Library in Weston, Ohio.

Yvette Johnson has been head of Children's Services at the Glenview Public Library in Glenview, Illinois, for the last fifteen years. Before this, she worked for the Chicago Public Library System. She was the head of the task force that recently revised the guidelines governing youth services in Illinois, *Managing Change,* published by the Illinois Library Association, 1993.

Sue McCleaf Nespeca is Youth Services coordinator for a consortium of more than eighty public, school, academic, and special libraries encompassing eight counties in Ohio. Presently convener for the Preschool Services Discussion Group, she has also served on the 1993 Caldecott Committee and as chair of the Publications and Preschool Services and Parent Education Committees. A contributor to the ALA publication *First Steps to Literacy: Library Programs for Parents, Teachers, and Caregivers*, she is also the author of *Library Programming for Families with Young Children: A How-to-Do-It Manual* (Neal-Schuman). Nespeca was the first recipient of the Bechtel Fellowship sponsored by the ALSC and the University of Florida.

In addition to planning continuing education opportunities for youth services librarians and coordinating county-wide projects for the fifty-four-member public libraries in the eastern half of Long Island, New York, **Marie C. Orlando** is active in promoting cooperation among agencies serving children and families. Formerly a children's librarian at the Shoreham-Wading River (N.Y.) Public Library, and a past president of the Children's Librarians Association of Suffolk County, Inc., she has served on the Executive Board of the Youth Services Section of the New York Library Association and is currently a member of the Managing Children's Services Committee of ALSC. She holds an M.L.S. from the Palmer School of Library and Information Science of Long Island University and has held management and board positions in business and in volunteer organizations, including the American Association of University Women.

Maria B. Salvadore began her career with the District of Columbia Public Library in Washington, D.C., where she worked in various positions serving diverse communities. Salvadore left D.C. Public to serve as coordinator of Children's Services for the Cambridge (Mass.) Public Library and returned to Washington, D.C., to become the coordinator of Children's Services, the position she currently holds.

Kathleen Staerkel heads the Young People's Services Department at the Indian Trails Public Library District in Wheeling, Illinois. There she presents workshops on customer service, telephone techniques, reference interviewing, and time management. She is actively involved in ALA/ALSC, the Illinois Library Association, and Illinois' North Suburban Library System. Recently, she co-authored *The Newbery and Caldecott Mock Election Kit: Choosing Champions in Children's Books* (American Library Association, 1994).

Kathy Toon has been employed by the Dallas Public Library for twenty-four years. She began her career as an assistant children's librarian until receiving her M.L.S. from the University of North Texas in 1978. Since then she has worked in branch libraries as a children's librarian, assistant branch manager, and branch manager. In 1987 she became division manager of the Children's Center of the J. Erik Jonsson Central library.

Mary M. Wagner is an associate professor at the College of St. Catherine in St. Paul, Minnesota. She teaches courses on library services to children and children's and young adult literature. She also plans and presents programs about children, their literature, and reading. She has worked in school and public libraries in the United States and Lesotho, Africa. Her research interests include the use of stories to acculturate children into groups and society.

Virginia Walter worked for more than twenty years in public libraries, most recently as Children's Services coordinator for Los Angeles Public Library, before joining the faculty at UCLA where she teaches courses in management and children's services. She is the author of *Output Measures for Public Library Service to Children* (American Library Association, 1992) and *War and Peace Literature for Children and Young Adults* (Oryx Press, 1993).

Gretchen M. Wronka is the senior librarian for Children's Services at Hennepin County Library in Minnetonka, Minnesota. She coordinates children's services for this suburban library system, which includes twenty-five agencies. She is a member of the Board of Directors for the ALSC (1993–95) and a past president of the Minnesota Library Association.

Index